| | |
|---|---|
| Parts of a boat | Nautical terms |
| Types of construction | Centre of effort |
| Safety at all times | Wind forces |
| Standing rigging | Resistance and balance |
| Running rigging | Tacking |
| Definitions | On a wind |
| The sails | Fresh conditions |
| Your first sail | Gybing |
| Getting under way — onshore winds | Balancing the boat |
| Effect of rudder | Rigging a spinnaker |

# LEARN TO SAIL

**FORTY EASY LESSONS WITH**
**LOU D'ALPUGET**

Illustrations by Jack Earl

VIKING O'NEIL

Viking O'Neil
Penguin Books Australia Ltd
487 Maroondah Highway, P.O. Box 257
Ringwood, Victoria 3134, Australia
Penguin Books Ltd
Harmondsworth, Middlesex, England
Viking Penguin Inc.
40 West 23rd Street, New York, N.Y. 10010, U.S.A.
Penguin Books Canada Limited
2801 John Street, Markham, Ontario, Canada L3R 1B4
Penguin Books (N.Z.) Ltd
182-190 Wairau Road, Auckland 10, New Zealand

First published as *Successful Sailing* by Thomas Nelson Australia 1970
Reprinted 1972, 1973, 1974
Revised paperback edition published 1981
This edition published by Penguin Books Australia 1989

10 9 8 7 6 5 4 3 2 1

Text copyright © Lou d'Alpuget, 1970, 1981
Illustrations copyright © Jack Earl, 1970

All rights reserved. Without limiting the rights under copyright reserved above, no part of this publication may be reproduced, stored in or introduced into a retrieval system, or transmitted, in any form or by any means (electronic, mechanical, photocopying, recording or otherwise) without the prior written permission of both the copyright owner and the above publisher of this book.

Produced by Viking O'Neil
56 Claremont Street, South Yarra, Victoria 3141, Australia
A division of Penguin Books Australia Ltd

Cover designed by R.T.J. Klinkhamer
Printed and bound in Hong Kong through Bookbuilders Ltd

National Library of Australia
Cataloguing-in-Publication data

d'Alpuget, Lou.
  Learn to sail.

  New ed.
  ISBN 0 670 90160 1.

  1. Sailing. I. Earl, Jack. II. d'Alpuget, Lou. Successful sailing. III. Title. IV. Title: Successful sailing.

797.1'24

# FOREWORD

Among the sounds that have a key to my memory in the enjoyment of boats and boating is the muffled quiet of the public library where I spent so many boyhood hours reading books about boats. The names of the authors flood back to me — Uffa Fox, Basil Lubbock, Arthur Ransome, Joseph Conrad — these were the great ones whom I read with awe.

But there was one little book I took down from the shelf again and again because for me it was crammed with pure enjoyment. It was full of beautiful action photographs of Australian high performance yachts and the text, though short, was a mine of information. This book was *Let's Go Sailing* by Lou d'Alpuget.

Many years later I met the author and he became one of my great friends. I had somehow imagined him as a thin, flamboyant Frenchman. Instead, I met a burly second-generation Australian, full of the quiet purposefulness and patience of the first-class seaman and navigator. He had been sailing all his life (indeed, well before I was born), racing and cruising in all types of boats from dinghies to some of Australia's largest yachts. He kept his own yacht in immaculate order . . .

Lou's background knowledge about boats and boating has become a byword among yachtsmen. His newspaper and magazine stories about the sport have inspired thousands of people to take it up and have been followed avidly by the most expert sailors. Apart from his way of telling a sailing story from the inside, the thing you can be sure about is that he has everything right, down to the last detail.

Now he has distilled a great deal of this meticulously accurate knowledge into yet another book, not mainly for the senses to enjoy this time, but a reference and text book.

The rawest beginner, who had never seen a boat, could read this book and from it learn to sail very well. All the steps are set out clearly, and are beautifully illustrated by the famous marine artist, Jack Earl.

The experienced yachtsman will also find the book of great value in helping him improve his techniques of boat handling and tuning. There are, in fact, a few pearls of wisdom that even the world's great yachtsmen would not be too proud to acknowledge as enlightening.

When Lou did me the honour to show me the final draft of this book I remarked: 'This could teach an Arab camel herdsman to sail.' But apart from learning from it, I hope everyone who reads it will also get as much enjoyment out of it as I did.

BEN LEXCEN
(from the Foreword to the first edition)

**The late Ben Lexcen, World and Australian sailing champion, was a dual Olympic representative and the designer of *Australia* II, winner of the America's Cup.**

# INTRODUCTION

Before you buy a boat you should consider carefully what you want from it.

Is it to be a simple dinghy you will use only until you have learnt to sail and will then exchange for a faster, more exciting craft?

Do you want to start in one of the family classes, like the Mirror or Heron dinghies?

Or are you willing to begin with a more demanding boat like a fibreglass Corsair?

If possible, talk to other people who have a boat of the type that attracts you and go sailing with them if they'll take you. It will help you to balance your ambition against reality.

And where and how will you store the boat when it is yours? In a rack in a club house, on a trailer in your front garden, in a corner of the garage or in a clear space under the house?

The boat should not be too big or too heavy for you and your crew to manhandle to and from the water without help, and the work of maintaining it in good order should not be so constant that you will find it a burden on your time.

The answers to all these questions are important to your enjoyment, so think about them seriously.

LOU D'ALPUGET

# CONTENTS

| | | |
|---|---|---|
| Foreword | | 2 |
| Introduction | | 3 |
| Lesson 1 | Parts of a boat | 4 |
| Lesson 2 | Types of construction | 6 |
| Lesson 3 | Safety at all times | 8 |
| Lesson 4 | Standing rigging | 10 |
| Lesson 5 | Running rigging | 12 |
| Lesson 6 | Definitions | 14 |
| Lesson 7 | The sails | 16 |
| Lesson 8 | Your first sail | 19 |
| Lesson 9 | Getting under way — onshore winds | 20 |
| Lesson 10 | Effect of rudder | 22 |
| Lesson 11 | Nautical terms | 24 |
| Lesson 12 | Centre of effort | 26 |
| Lesson 13 | Wind forces | 27 |
| Lesson 14 | Resistance and balance | 28 |
| Lesson 15 | Tacking | 29 |
| Lesson 16 | On a wind | 30 |
| Lesson 17 | Fresh conditions | 31 |
| Lesson 18 | Gybing | 32 |
| Lesson 19 | Balancing the boat | 34 |
| Lesson 20 | Rigging a spinnaker | 37 |
| Lesson 21 | Setting a spinnaker | 38 |
| Lesson 22 | Spinnaker trimming | 42 |
| Lesson 23 | Gybing and lowering a spinnaker | 44 |
| Lesson 24 | Sails and sail handling | 46 |
| Lesson 25 | Setting up the mainsail | 48 |
| Lesson 26 | Leech adjustments | 50 |
| Lesson 27 | Camber of mainsails | 52 |
| Lesson 28 | Adjusting mainsheet — light conditions | 54 |
| Lesson 29 | Adjusting mainsheet — fresh conditions | 56 |
| Lesson 30 | Headsails and their uses | 58 |
| Lesson 31 | Overlapping headsails | 60 |
| Lesson 32 | Setting up headsails | 62 |
| Lesson 33 | Shape of headsails | 64 |
| Lesson 34 | Trimming headsails | 66 |
| Lesson 35 | Masts | 68 |
| Lesson 36 | Heavy winds | 70 |
| Lesson 37 | Backstay adjustments | 72 |
| Lesson 38 | Controlling mast bends | 74 |
| Lesson 39 | Side bends | 76 |
| Lesson 40 | Mast shapes | 78 |
| Major knots, Metric conversion table | | 79 |
| Glossary | | 80 |

# LESSON 1
## Parts of a boat

Learning to sail a boat is like learning to play a piano: the basic essentials are simple but it takes time, study and lots of practice before you become proficient.

A sailing boat is a complicated machine. There is no sense in pretending otherwise. It is influenced by the ever-changing direction and strength of the wind and by the way the sails are trimmed to suit these changes. It is influenced also by the direction and depth of the waves and even by ripples on the surface of the water as well as by where you put your weight.

So, before we start learning the various techniques for controlling a boat, let us examine the parts of one, together with the special names given to these parts and to boating equipment. These names may seem strange at first because they have little relation to things ashore. But when it is realised that they are precise names, given to nothing else, you will appreciate how easy it is to recognise them and so to avoid confusion.

The illustrations show details of a dinghy, a simple little plywood boat and an ideal one in which to learn to sail. It is called a **hard-chine dinghy** because a strip of timber called a **chine** is used to secure its almost flat bottom to the sides at a definite angle. Lately, fibreglass tape and epoxy resin have been used for the same purpose.

Now study closely all the parts of the boat and its equipment until you can remember their names and recognise them at a glance.

The 4.26m Skate class is a larger version of the Australian-developed Vee Jay and, although there are not many sailing, their devotees find them an exciting and challenging boat to ride. They carry sliding planks on their decks to allow helmsman and crew to swing their bodies full length over the side in hard winds. *WA Newspapers*

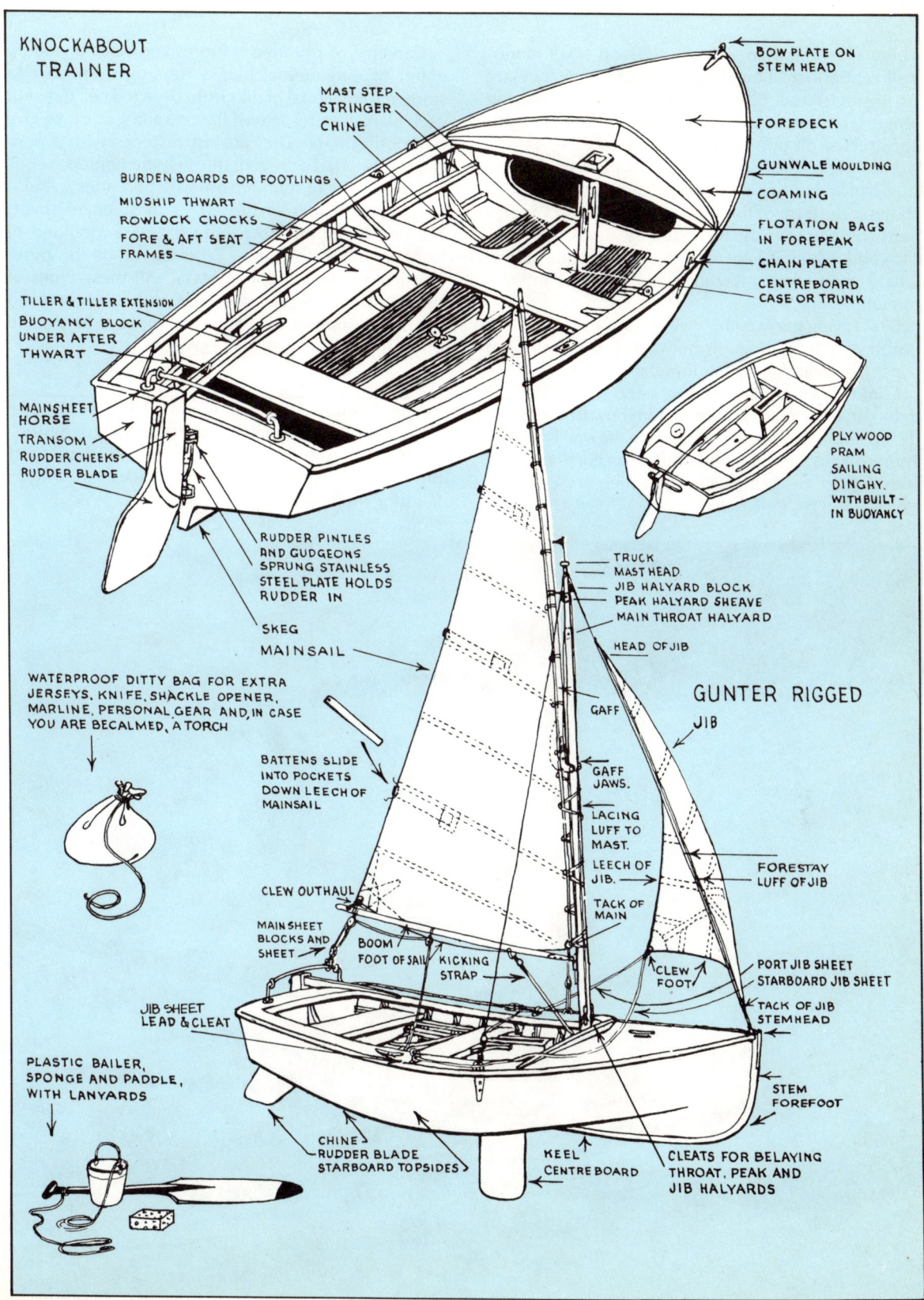

# LESSON 2
# Types of construction

There are more than sixteen thousand small monohull centreboard boats sailing in Australia. They are of 67 registered different classes, and of varying lengths, hull shapes and sail plans. All, however, are constructed on one of four basic principles.

We have already shown the layout and equipment of a typical hard-chine dinghy. (Our next illustration shows a close-up of this type of construction.) Such a hard-chine boat is usually made of sheets of marine plywood, which is light and strong. The outer skin of a hard-chine dinghy is usually supported by internal frames.

By studying the accompanying illustrations you will find it easy to distinguish between this principle of construction and the other three, which are:

**Clinker:** of rounded bottoms and sides, made up of longitudinal planks running from bow to stern with the edge of each plank overlapping the one below it. These planks can be glued and/or fastened together with copper rivets through ribs which are correctly called **timbers**.

**Carvel:** of rounded bottoms and sides, made up either of longitudinal planks running from bow to stern or of diagonal planks from deck to keel, but with each plank butting against the one alongside it, to give a smooth surface. They are also fastened with copper rivets (clenched or roved) through the timbers.

**Moulded:** of rounded bottoms and sides and also of angular shapes, made up of thin veneer sheets bonded together. Most these days are moulded of fibreglass but they may also be made of other plastics or pressed out of metal. All these types of moulded construction are light and strong and do not need supporting frames or timbers as do the other three.

---

The unsinkable Vaucluse Junior (3.5m) was once the most popular boat in Australia for youngsters learning to sail but it has gradually been developed into a sophisticated, high-performance craft, a little daunting for most beginners.

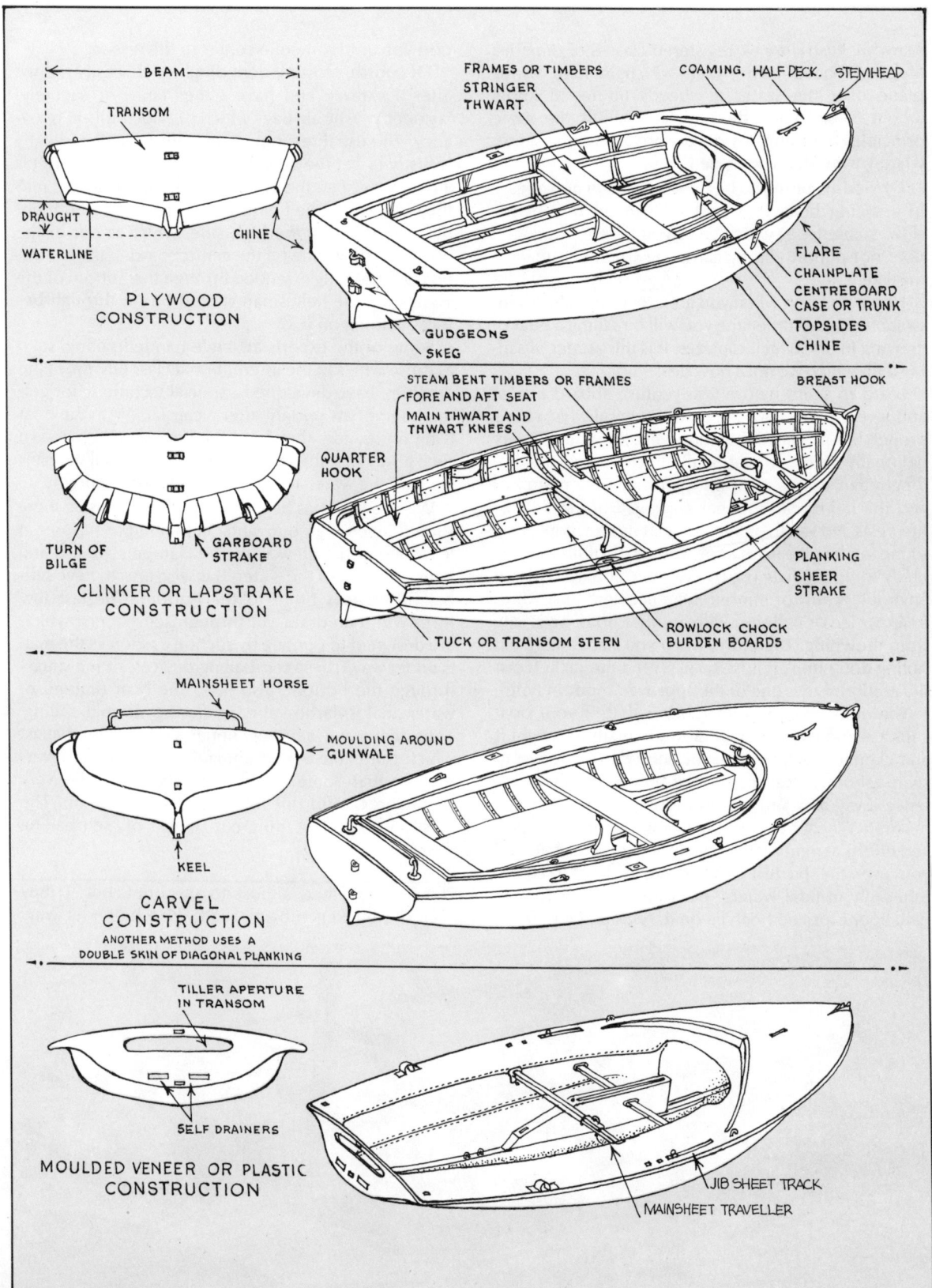

# LESSON 3
## Safety at all times

Many of Australia's 67 registered classes of dinghies are high-speed racing craft which in hard winds plane over the water at speeds up to 18 knots (about 33 kph) for short distances. But the basic principles of sailing any dinghy are always the same, whatever its size and speed.

Obviously, until you become proficient and at ease in a sailing boat, it is best to learn in one of the slow, stable types which gives you time to think and does not punish you by capsizing when you make a mistake.

However, even when you are expert, it is almost inevitable that at some time you will be sailing a boat or crewing in one which capsizes. It is this aspect of sailing with which we must now deal.

Learn to swim before you venture aboard a boat and, even if you are a good swimmer, always wear a proper life-jacket or flotation vest. In almost every nationally and internationally recognised class of dinghy racing it is compulsory for all crew members and the helmsman to wear approved life-jackets or life-vests. No yacht, no matter what its size, is allowed to race unless it carries approved types of life-jackets ready for immediate use by everyone aboard. Then, if anybody is hurt or injured in an accident aboard, or in a capsize or collision with another boat, he is safe from drowning. Therefore, when you start small boat sailing don't think it is 'sissy' to wear a life-jacket: our illustration shows one of the approved modern types.

The other thing to remember is that, if your boat capsizes and you and your crew are unable to right it and clamber back aboard, you should not attempt to swim ashore, unless the shore is only a very short distance away and you are absolutely certain you can make it. When wet clothing has weighed you down and efforts at righting the boat have already exhausted you, even the shortest distance may be hard to cover, especially in tidal waters. The safest thing is to stay with your capsized boat, lie on it, relax and let it support you until someone comes to the rescue.

Of course, most modern dinghies are easily righted after a capsize and have either tanks or securely-fastened plastic air-bags which provide built-in buoyancy. The usual technique for righting such a dinghy is firstly to get the bow pointing into the wind: if it is a two-man boat, the crewman can hold the boat into the wind while the helmsman levers the hull upright by holding on to the high side, which is out of the water, and standing on the centreboard. If the centreboard is not fully extended through the bottom of the boat, then the helmsman should pull it through before standing on it.

Some of the experts at single-handed sailing, such as those who sail the international class Olympic Finn dinghies, have developed a special technique for getting their boats upright after a capsize. With the boat lying on its side, they hold the bow head to wind in such a way that the wind flows under the sail which is lying on the water and flicks the boat back upright.

When a boat has been righted after a capsize there should be enough buoyancy in the hull to support at least one of the crew while he clambers aboard and bails out most of the water. It is wise also to have self-bailing devices fitted to the bottom. The last few litres will then drain out through self-bailers, which are designed to operate by suction as soon as the boat is under way. These self-bailing devices, fitting snugly through the bottom, also keep the boat drained of water that splashes aboard during normal sailing. Thus they save carrying unnecessary water ballast which can make a boat unmanageable. Note, nevertheless, that some metal self-bailers may be very sharp; be careful not to cut yourself on them. The illustrations show different types of self-bailing devices.

---

They've filled her, almost to the brim, but if they keep the buckets moving she'll soon be under way.

1. AFTER CAPSIZE, CREWMAN HOLDING BOW ACTS AS A DROGUE, BRINGING BOAT'S HEAD TO WIND. SKIPPER STANDING ON CENTREBOARD, LEVERS DINGHY UP

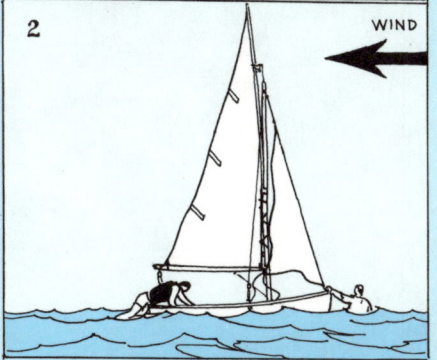
2. CREWMAN REMAINS HOLDING BOW, SKIPPER SLIDES ABOARD AFT, SHUTS OFF THE SELF-BAILER...

3. ...AND BAILS OUT THE BULK OF WATER.

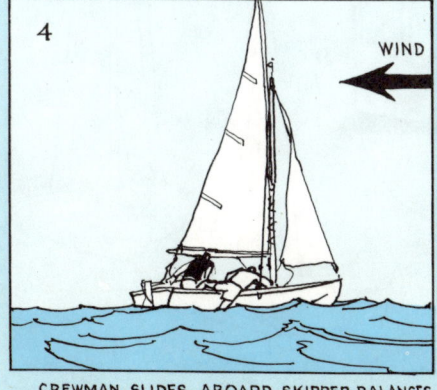
4. CREWMAN SLIDES ABOARD, SKIPPER BALANCES THE BOAT TO COUNTER HIS WEIGHT

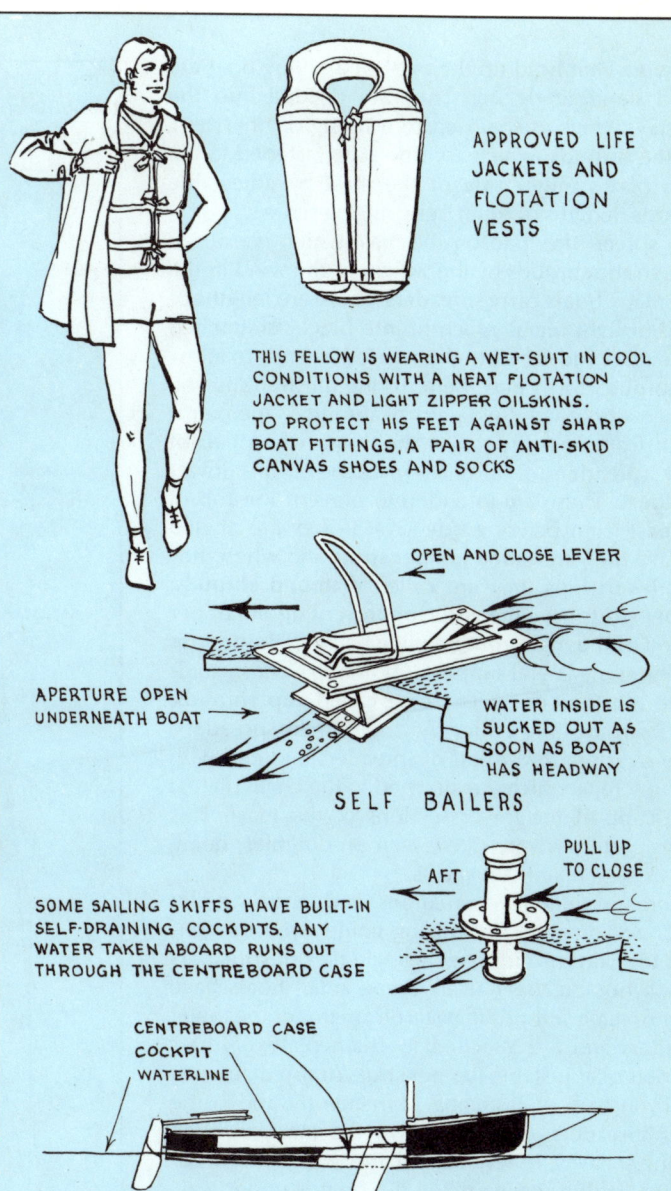

APPROVED LIFE JACKETS AND FLOTATION VESTS

THIS FELLOW IS WEARING A WET-SUIT IN COOL CONDITIONS WITH A NEAT FLOTATION JACKET AND LIGHT ZIPPER OILSKINS. TO PROTECT HIS FEET AGAINST SHARP BOAT FITTINGS, A PAIR OF ANTI-SKID CANVAS SHOES AND SOCKS

SELF BAILERS

OPEN AND CLOSE LEVER
APERTURE OPEN UNDERNEATH BOAT
WATER INSIDE IS SUCKED OUT AS SOON AS BOAT HAS HEADWAY

PULL UP TO CLOSE
AFT

SOME SAILING SKIFFS HAVE BUILT-IN SELF-DRAINING COCKPITS. ANY WATER TAKEN ABOARD RUNS OUT THROUGH THE CENTREBOARD CASE

CENTREBOARD CASE
COCKPIT
WATERLINE

THEY HAVE TREMENDOUS BUILT-IN BUOYANCY, ARE FAST TO RIGHT AND BE UNDER WAY AGAIN. WHEN CAPSIZED IN HEAVY WINDS HOWEVER THEY CAN BLOW AWAY TO LEEWARD FASTER THAN THE CREW CAN SWIM, SO KEEP HOLD OF YOUR VESSEL

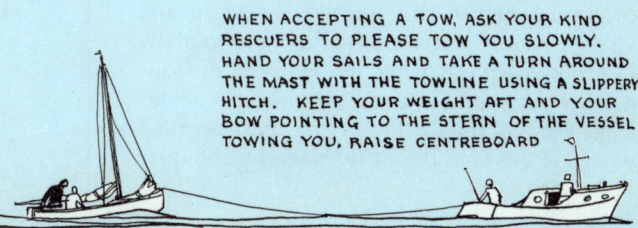

WHEN ACCEPTING A TOW, ASK YOUR KIND RESCUERS TO PLEASE TOW YOU SLOWLY. HAND YOUR SAILS AND TAKE A TURN AROUND THE MAST WITH THE TOWLINE USING A SLIPPERY HITCH. KEEP YOUR WEIGHT AFT AND YOUR BOW POINTING TO THE STERN OF THE VESSEL TOWING YOU. RAISE CENTREBOARD

# LESSON 4
# Standing rigging

The wires that hold up the mast of a sailing boat are called **standing rigging**. They are divided into the **forestay**, which is shackled to a fitting on the stem, and the **shrouds**, which are side stays fastened to the chain plates either side of the mast by adjustable **lanyards** (lengths of rope) or by rigging screws.

To spread the load on the mast which is exerted through the shrouds by the weight of the wind in the sails, many boats carry **spreaders**. These are lengths of wood or light metal which fit into brackets attached to the mast and are slotted on the outer ends to allow the shrouds to fit into them. In the illustrations you will see a boat with two pairs of shrouds. One pair is rigged from near the top of the mast, over a pair of small spreaders, and ends just above the lower spreaders. These are intended to prevent the top of the mast from bending sideways: if they are angled forward they are called **jumper struts** and when they are athwartships they are called **diamond shrouds**. Jumper struts have the virtue of preventing the upper section of the mast from bending backwards, besides lending some lateral support. Another pair of shrouds in the illustrations, in this case called **cap shrouds**, start from a fitting under the top pair of spreaders, travel over the lower pair of spreaders and end with rigging screws which are attached to the chain plates; these support the lower sections of the mast. This rigging system is very rarely seen on dinghies, being used instead mainly on yachts.

There are numerous variations, and in the simpler beginners' dinghies the rigging could even be confined to main shrouds over a single pair of spreaders or with no spreaders at all. Some small boats have lower or main shrouds that start from under the lower spreaders and are attached to chain plates. Others have sets of adjustable jumper struts or top diamonds which, instead of fastening permanently above the lower spreaders, continue down the mast, through guiding sheaves, to levers and cams which allow adjustment of the rigging when the boat is under way. Some high-speed racing craft also have their cap shrouds, lower shrouds and forestays attached to adjustable cams, levers and winching systems. But essentially all these methods of rigging a mast have one thing in common—they are designed to keep it upright.

The adjustments on the forestay, backstay and shrouds of a racing boat are intended only to allow the mast to be bent to change the shape of the sails to suit varying strengths of wind and different angles of sailing. We will discuss controlled mast bending later when we are considering advanced techniques of sail trimming.

Time spent ashore carefully rigging your boat ensures that you know every detail of its equipment and how to adjust it in an emergency.

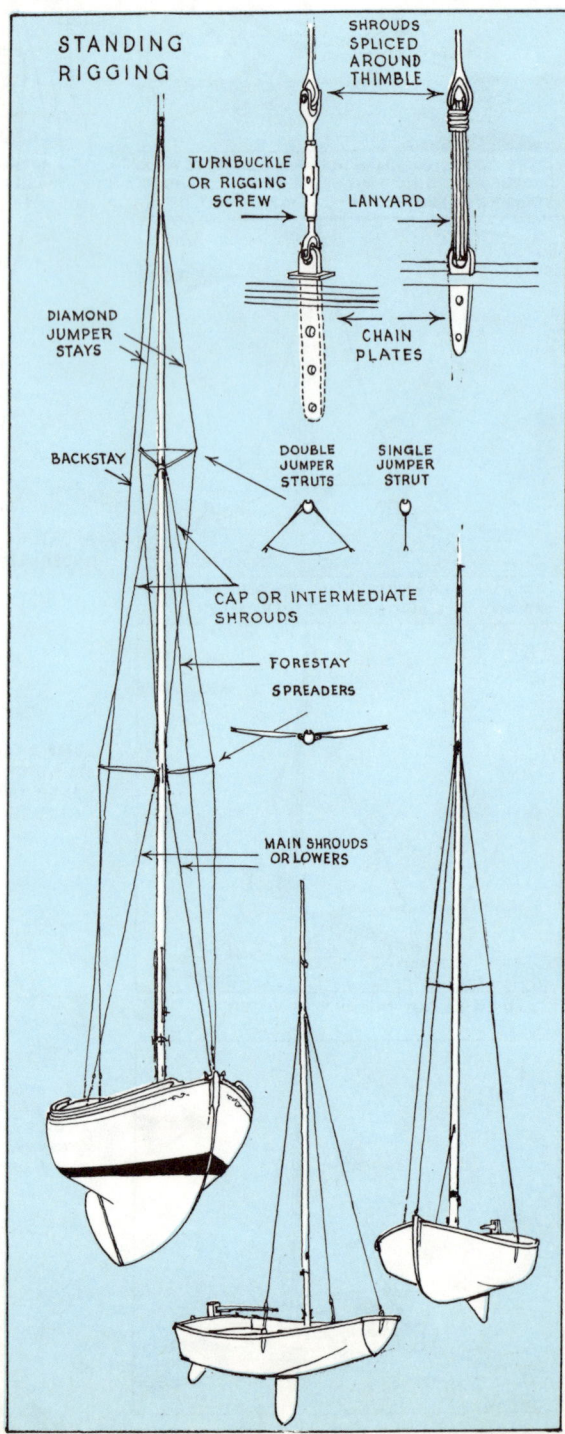

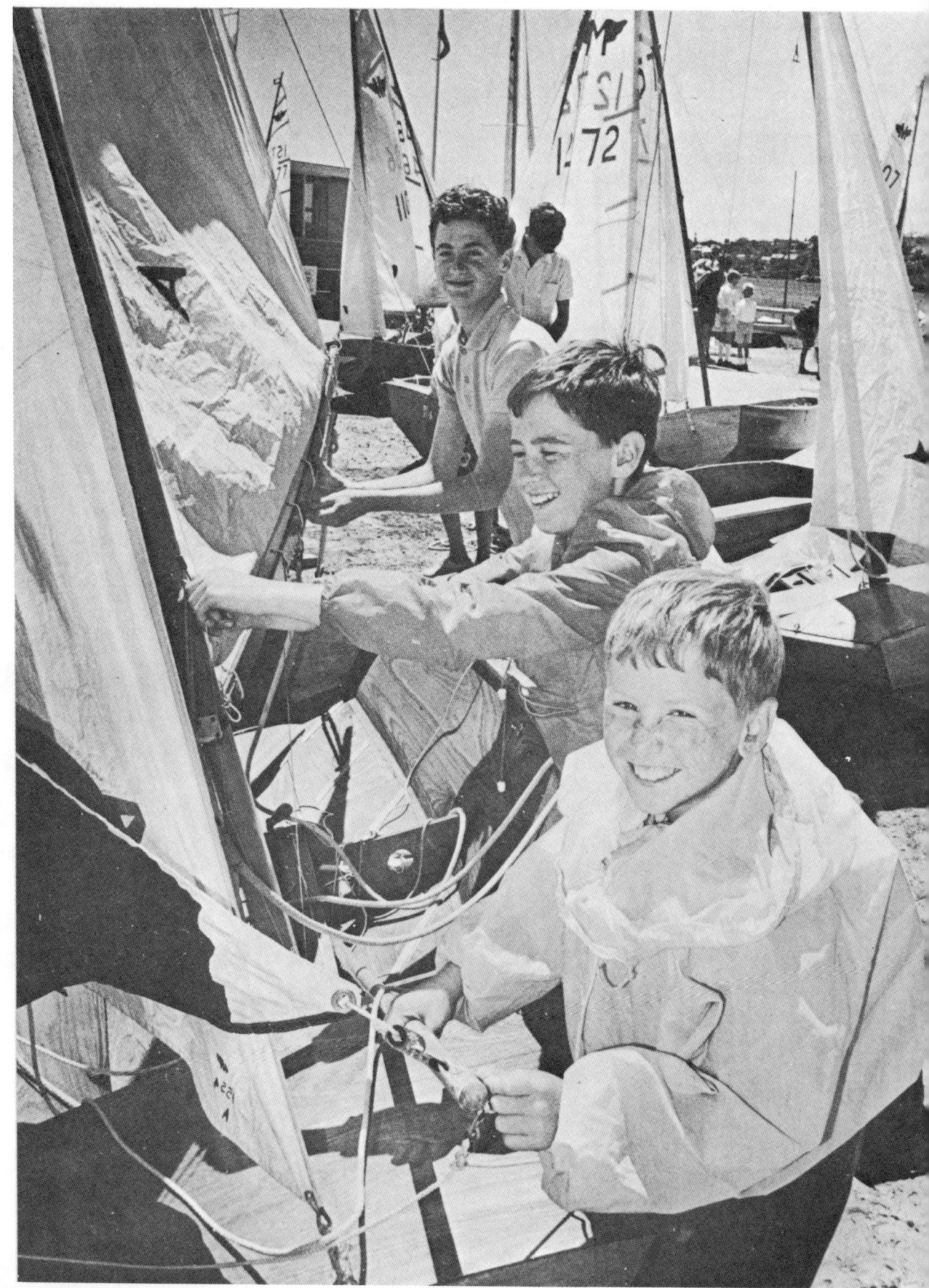

# LESSON 5
# Running rigging

The wires and ropes which haul up and hold up the sails are called **running rigging**.

They are **halyards** (or halliards), named from the days of the old square-rigged sailing ship, when the yards (great spars to which the sails were attached) had to be hauled into place by ropes.

There are two halyards on the normal sloop-rigged dinghy—i.e. a dinghy which has only one foresail (the **jib**) in front of the mast. One halyard, for hauling up and holding up the jib, is called the jib halyard; the other, for hauling up and holding up the mainsail, the large triangular sail behind the mast, is called the main halyard.

The other ropes on the boat in the illustration are called **sheets**, used for pulling the sails tight or for easing them off, depending on the angle at which one is sailing to the wind. The jib sheets are fastened to the **clew** of the jib and led to either side of the boat thence back through **fairleads** into the cockpit: the mainsheet is fastened to the boom and led through mainsheet blocks, one end of which is attached to the mainsheet horse and also led back into the cockpit.

On a simple sailing dinghy each halyard is led through a **block** (a wooden, metal or plastic shell containing a **sheave**, or wheel, over which a rope may run) and down the mast to a horned **cleat** (see illustration) to which it is fastened. On modern racing dinghies and on racing yachts, especially those with hollow metal masts, the halyards are led down inside the mast and out of an exit box to a cam-cleat. Some racing dinghies dispense with a main halyard altogether and have the top (or head) of their mainsail clipped or locked to the top of their mast. (To rig a mainsail of this type it is, of course, necessary to lay the boat over on its side when it is ashore.)

The rope sheets can be of hemp, cotton or of synthetic fibres—nylon, terylene, dacron or polypropylene—and they may be cable-laid (in three distinct strands coiled around each other), plaited or braided (in a varying number of interlocking strands). Although hemp is easy to splice it becomes very hard and difficult to handle when wet, and though cotton is soft it stretches excessively and is liable to rot. On modern boats, sheets of synthetic fibres are most popular and are used almost universally: although expensive, they are very strong, wear well, are rot-proof and easy to clean.

There's a friendly spirit of cooperation among sailors of all ages. Never hesitate to ask a fellow club member for guidance.

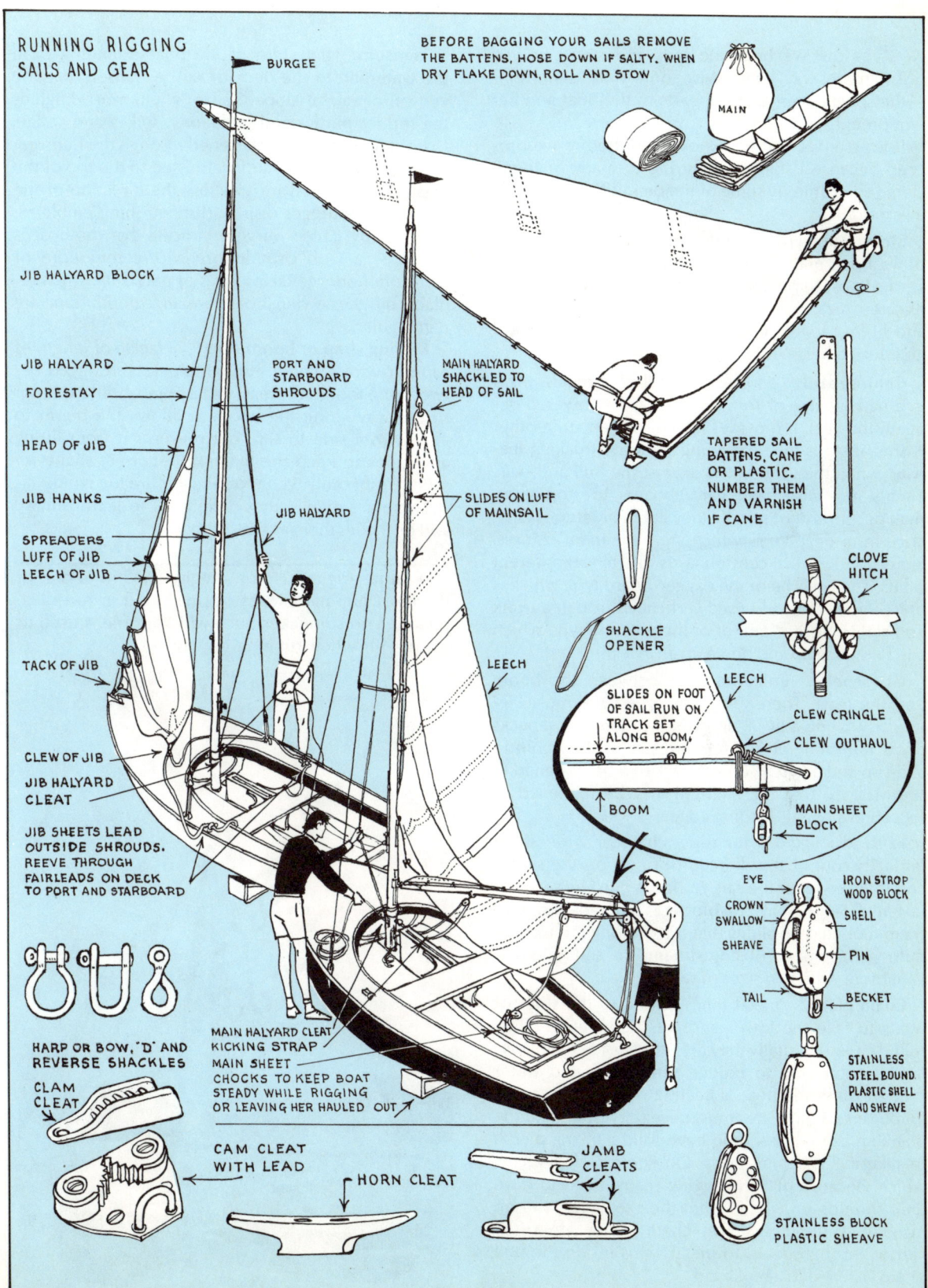

# LESSON 6
## Definitions

Now, before we hoist the sails and start our first lesson under way, let us revise some of the definitions —the special names of the parts of the boat and her equipment.

It is essential that you know them before we proceed because I shall be referring to many of them. Here I shall amplify some of the definitions and add a few more.

**Stem:** upwards continuation of the keel at the bows. Boats may be straight-stemmed, with an almost vertical post joining the keel, or there may be a complicated arrangement of sections scarfed (jointed) and bolted together or laminated in thin strips and glued together.

**Centreboard:** a wood or metal or fibreglass plate in a narrow case or trunk which can be lowered beneath the keel. It provides lateral resistance; in other words, it stops the boat going sideways (making **leeway**) when the wind blows against the hull and sails. Yachts may also have centreboards to stop them making leeway but usually they get their lateral resistance from deep keels which are permanent fixtures. Shapes and sizes of centreboards vary to suit different boats. They may be of the dagger-board type which is merely lowered and raised vertically through a trunk and slot in the bottom, or of the pivoting type which can be swung up and down on an axle pin.

**Gooseneck:** universal joint between the boom and the mast. There are many types, the most elementary being a hook and eye. Modern goosenecks allow the fitting on the forward end of the boom to slide up and down a vertical track or a bar fastened to the mast, so that the mainsail may be tightened or loosened along its leading edge.

**Fairleads:** guides for rope, chain or wire; sheet fairleads control the direction of pull on the sheets and thus the set of the sail. Fairleads must be securely fastened. Some boats use blocks as fairleads and have them mounted on slides that travel along tracks, permitting a number of adjustments to suit different weights of wind and sizes of sail.

**Chain plates:** metal tangs bolted to the sides of boats to take the lower ends of the shrouds (illustrated earlier). Usually they are fitted inside the planking or outer skin to reduce turbulence and water friction when the boat is heeling over with her side immersed. Chain plates must never be fastened to the planking alone but should have solid packing pieces to take the fastening bolts. On some racing yachts which, because of their rigging plans, need to have their shrouds set well in from their topsides, and on many ocean-going yachts, chain plates are often carried through decks to metal webs inside the hull or are fastened to a bulkhead.

**Transom:** flat stern of the boat extending from the waterline to the deck or rail. A transom may be vertical or raked (sloped) slightly. On most dinghies the rudder **pintles** and **gudgeons** (spikes and collars to hold the rudder) are fastened through the transom.

**Burgee:** a triangular flag hoisted to the top of the mast on a flag halyard to show the direction of the wind. Club burgees display distinguishing emblems, and swallow-tailed burgees indicate that the boat is sailed by a club commodore, vice-commodore or rear-commodore. Racing flags or pennants which replace burgees when boats are in competition, are rectangular.

**Kicking strap** or **boom vang:** a tackle or length of rope or wire running through blocks and rigged between the foot of the mast and a point about a quarter of the way along the boom. It allows the boom to swing from side to side but prevents it from lifting and helps to keep the mainsail in correct shape for sailing, especially when running before the wind.

There are many other definitions to learn but we will deal with them as they arise.

---

The gunter-rigged Heron dinghy (3.43m) is one of the most popular classes of small boat in Australia. It carries no spinnaker but a whisker pole is used to set the jib when running downwind.

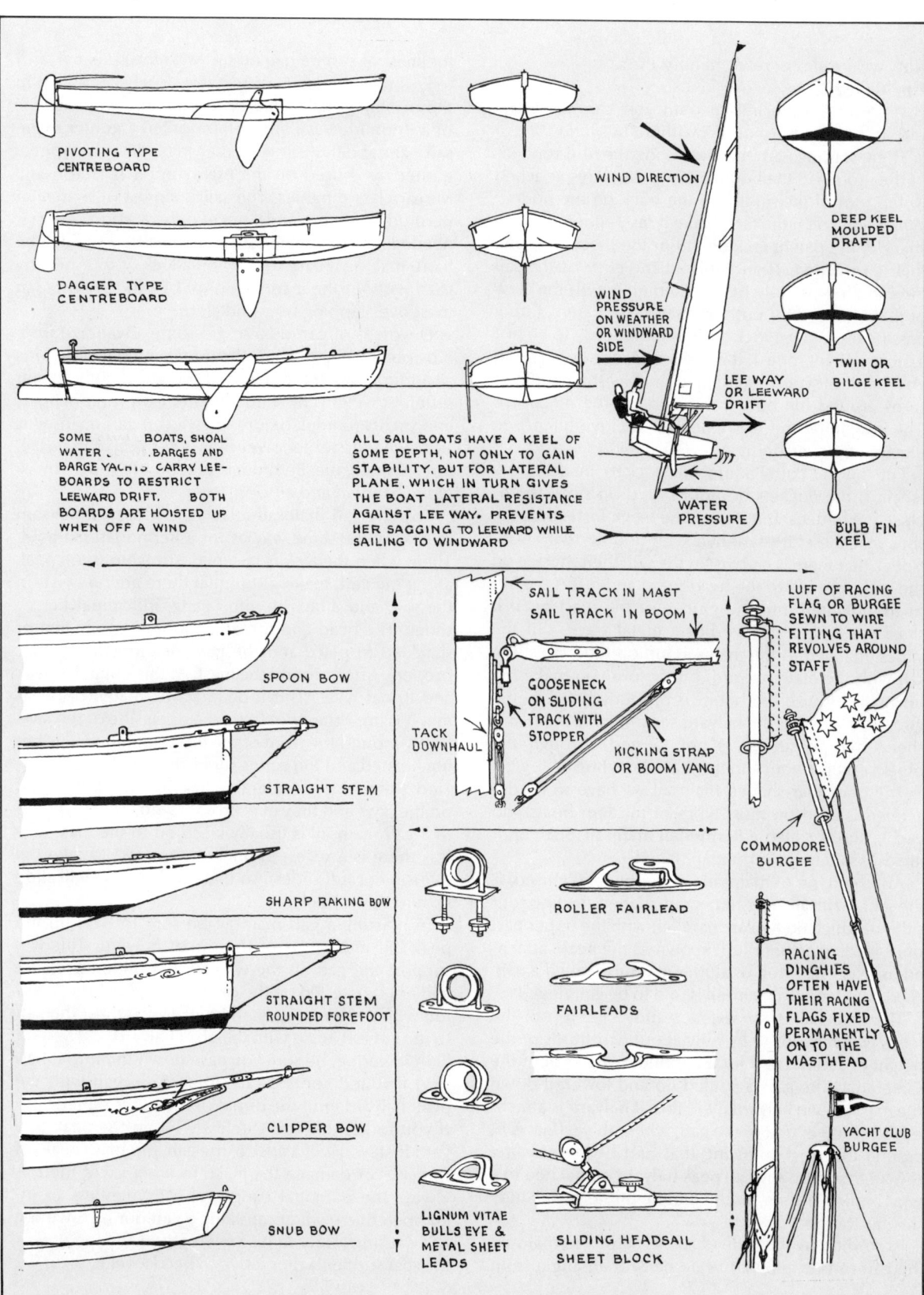

# LESSON 7
## The sails

Now we are almost ready to hoist the sails.
**The Mainsail**
First study the illustration until you can name the various parts of the mainsail without hesitation.

Then, starting with the clew, slide the foot rope into the groove in the boom (or slip the slides attached to the foot of the sail on to the track on the boom). When you reach the tack make it fast, either with the shackle, the patent locking pin or the piece of lacing that is provided. Then haul out the clew of the sail until the foot is fairly tight, fastening it with the clew outhaul. This clew outhaul may be a patent fitting passing through a block but it is more likely to be just a piece of light rope. If it is a piece of rope be sure that you finish off your fastening with at least a couple of turns around the boom and through the metal eye (the **cringle**) at the clew; tie with a clove hitch (see illustration in lesson five).

Put the sail battens into the pockets made in the leech. If the pockets do not have 'drop slots' to enclose the battens, but ties on the leech instead, make sure that these are fastened with double reef knots. Check that there is no twist in the sail, then shackle on the main halyard to the headboard and insert the luff of the mainsail into the groove of the mast or, if it does not have a groove but a metal track, slip the slides attached to the mainsail luff on to it. Hoist the sail with the main halyard, but before you make the luff tight be sure the boom is properly fitted to the gooseneck. Fasten the halyard securely. Rig the mainsheet, making sure it is not twisted, through the blocks on the boom and the mainsheet horse.

The triangular-shaped mainsail we have so far described is used on most types of modern boats and yachts and is called a **Bermudan mainsail**. Such craft are thus said to be Bermudan rigged.

Another type of mainsail, once universally used, is the **gaff mainsail**: it is trapezoid-shaped (having four sides of which no two are parallel) with the upper part of its leading edge or luff, known as the **peak**, attached to a spar of wood or aluminium tube called a **gaff**. A boat with such a mainsail is said to be gaff rigged.

The detachable gaff extends above the top of the mast, which needs to be only about two-thirds of the height of a mast used for a Bermudan mainsail of the same area. The gaff is hauled up and lowered down the mast by two halyards; the **throat halyard** is attached to the lower end of the gaff, where the gaff jaws fit around the mast, allowing that part of the sail (the throat) to rotate, and the **peak halyard** is attached to a wire bridle (or sling) in the middle of the gaff. (Study the illustration.)

According to the individual shape of the mainsail the gaff can be allowed to lie back at an angle from the mast or can be hauled up (with the peak halyard) to lie snugly against it. When it is closely hauled up to the mast, the mainsail may take up almost the shape of a Bermudan sail and is then called a **gunter mainsail**. The boat is thus gunter rigged. This type of gunter rig is used on the highly popular Heron and Mirror class dinghies. The sail is almost of triangular Bermudan shape and, since only a short mast is needed, this and the gaff can be fitted inside the boat, making it easy to stow on a rack or transport by road without the inconvenience of a long Bermudan mast over-lapping bow and stern.

Devotees of gaff rig also get some advantage from it by being able to adjust the throat and peak halyards and thus change the shape of the sail slightly to suit different weights of wind. Theoretically, on big boats and yachts running before the wind, a gaff mainsail is somewhat easier to lower than a Bermudan mainsail. But, overall, the Bermudan mainsail is much more easily handled and efficient.

To rig a gaff mainsail attach the foot to the boom in exactly the same way as for a Bermudan mainsail. Then, when the tack is fastened, stretch out the peak along the gaff, making sure that there are no twists in the sail, and attach it with lacing, individual ties or slides. The head and throat must be securely tied or shackled in place and the jaws of the gaff must be properly fitted around the mast. At this stage the peak and throat halyards can be attached ready for hoisting. It is important *not* to tie the open side of the jaws firmly around the front of the mast until the sail is being hoisted and the gaff is supported by the peak halyard, otherwise considerable leverage will be exerted on the jaws and they may be damaged. The lower luff of a gaff mainsail is usually laced on to the mast (unless there is a recessed track in the mast to take the luff rope or luff slides), so that the gaff jaws will slide up and down freely.

In hoisting a gaff mainsail be sure to haul up the peak halyard *ahead* of the throat halyard. This will support the gaff all the way so that undue pressure will not be exerted on the gaff jaws. Tighten the lower luff with the throat halyard before you adjust the gaff to the correct angle with the peak halyard.

In lowering, be sure you ease down the throat halyard first and continue to support the gaff with the peak halyard until the throat of the sail is right down. If you forget this and carelessly let go the peak halyard first, you will 'capsize' the gaff and may break off the jaws or damage the mast. In a big yacht there is always the potential danger of a thoughtless or incompetent crewman capsizing a gaff during lowering and causing injury to his crewmates if the top end of the spar suddenly dips down to head level.

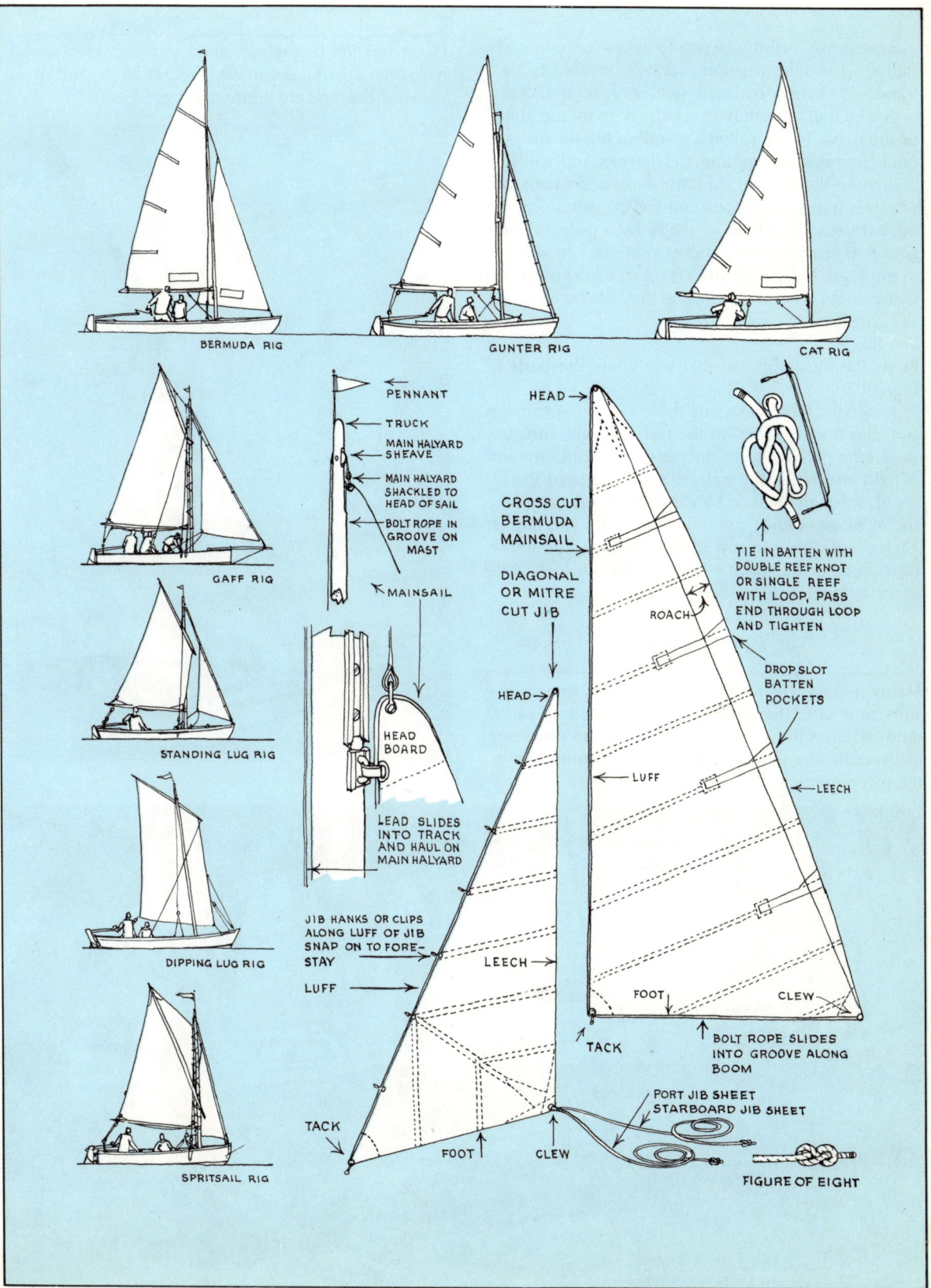

Before we finish discussing types of mainsails, perhaps I should mention that it is possible to rig a trapezoid-shaped mainsail with only one halyard, provided that the gaff is long enough to jut out ahead of the mast. This is called a **standing lug rig** and was once popular on commercial barges and cruising boats (see illustration). Another type is the **sprit sail**, which is trapezoid-shaped but has no gaff along the peak. Instead it is held in shape by a pole called a sprit that extends from a socket in the tack to another in the head. Neither of these is much used nowadays, except as an emergency rig, and they can be regarded as curiosities.

**The Jib**

Study the illustration so that you know the parts of the sail

Fasten the tack, make sure there are no twists in the sail, clip the jib hanks on the luff on to the forestay, fasten the jib halyard to the head, hoist until the luff is tight and fasten the halyard securely. Lead the jib sheets through the lead blocks or bulls-eyes and tie a figure of eight knot (see illustration) on the end of each sheet. This prevents it slipping back through its lead block or bulls-eye when it is let run free while you are under way.

Once hoisted a well-designed gaff rigged mainsail has some advantages in certain conditions but most yachts these days are Bermudan rigged.

Manly Juniors, ideal 2.58m training boats for youngsters, are safe, buoyant and can be used as yacht tenders. From these, hundreds graduate to the more lively skiffs like the Cherub under shy spinnaker in the foreground.

# LESSON 8
## Your first sail

Choose a day when the breeze is very light, i.e. no more than 10 knots, for your first sail. If possible, the spot from which you launch your boat should be a gently sloping shore or slipway. It is also a good idea to have someone with experience standing by, if not actively to help, at least to supervise.

Before you 'bend on' your sails, hoist up your burgee on the flag halyard in order to find the direction of the wind. Then turn the bow of the boat into the wind and hoist the sails as detailed in Lesson 7. Be sure that the jib sheets and the mainsheet run freely and fasten down the kicking strap so that the boom will not lift. Check that the boat's buoyancy bags are in order and that the drain plugs or corks are in.

Remember, on your first few tries, not to venture too far away from the shore. The water near the shore, so long as it is clear of rocks and sandbanks, is just as good for learning to sail and much less dangerous than 2 km out. Another policy in the early stages *in onshore winds* is to head up as near as practicable to the wind if you get into trouble. Then, according to the shape of the waterway and the land mass around it, you will always drift ashore.

**Getting Under Way—Offshore and Parallel Winds**

Getting under way with an offshore wind (one which is blowing from the shore to the water), or with a wind that is blowing parallel to the shore is very easy, although it does not really matter where the wind blows from if you follow the correct procedures.
*Offshore and parallel winds*

Manoeuvre the boat into water about half a metre deep so that it will float easily with the rudder blade clear of the bottom: have your crewman hold the bow so that it does not swing away from the wind. Now the helmsman should climb aboard and fit the rudder so that the pintles and gudgeons are properly engaged. It is also wise to tie the rudder with a light piece of rope so that it won't lift out and float away if you capsize. He should then slip the tiller into position, making sure that its holding pin is in place and that it cannot slide out accidentally. The centreboard at this stage *should be kept raised* so that it is clear of the bottom but ready for lowering as soon as the water is deep enough.

The crewman can now give the boat a shove out into deeper water and at the same time clamber aboard. If he wishes he can wade out with the boat, still holding its bows to the wind—but he must be ready to get aboard smartly. While the crewman is getting aboard, the helmsman must balance the boat to prevent it capsizing or taking any water over the side. The sheets must be left free and the sails should still be flapping.

Before the wind fills the sails, the boat, under the impetus of the crewman's push, will probably still be moving astern, so the helmsman must now turn the rudder to steer the boat astern. To do this when the boat is moving backwards he must point the blade of the rudder in the direction he wishes the stern to travel.

In this case, with an offshore or a parallel wind, since it will be desirable to have the bows pointing away from the shore, it will be necessary to steer the stern of the boat slightly towards the shore.

Helmsman and crew can now gradually haul on the sheets to stop the boat moving astern and to start moving it ahead.

Then the helmsman should steer the boat 'by the bow' instead of 'by the stern' to keep heading in the right direction.

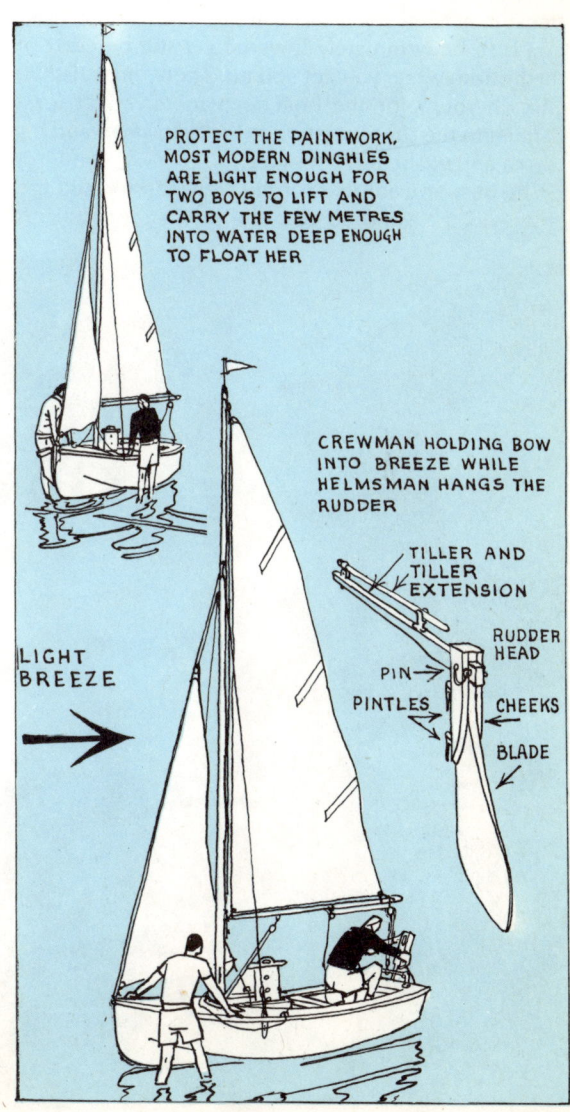

PROTECT THE PAINTWORK. MOST MODERN DINGHIES ARE LIGHT ENOUGH FOR TWO BOYS TO LIFT AND CARRY THE FEW METRES INTO WATER DEEP ENOUGH TO FLOAT HER

CREWMAN HOLDING BOW INTO BREEZE WHILE HELMSMAN HANGS THE RUDDER

TILLER AND TILLER EXTENSION
RUDDER HEAD
PIN
PINTLES
CHEEKS
BLADE

LIGHT BREEZE

# LESSON 9
# Getting under way – onshore winds

If the boat is at first slow to 'pay off' in the direction you wish to sail, that is, if it continues to lie 'head to the wind', the crewman may have to 'back' the jib. To do this he holds out the clew of the jib on the side of the boat opposite the direction in which it is to be set until it fills with wind and swings the bow around. Then he must let the clew go and haul gradually on the jib sheet on the side the sail is setting.

As soon as the boat is moving, the centreboard can be lowered, but only gradually, until the water is deep enough for it to project fully under the keel.

To get under way with an onshore wind, one that blows from the water to the land, the early preparations are the same as for offshore and parallel winds. You must keep the boat's bow pointing into the wind, but you must also take the boat into water deep enough to allow the rudder to be shipped when the transom is nearest the shore and to allow the centreboard to be completely lowered yet still be clear of the bottom when you get aboard. There must also be enough room for the boat to manoeuvre, at least parallel to the shore, as soon as the helmsman and his crewman get aboard.

The best procedure is for the crewman to hold the bow into the wind so that the sails cannot fill on either side: if they did so at this stage they could force the boat to bear away and travel back inshore into shallow water. The helmsman should then get aboard, make sure that the rudder is properly fitted, slide in the tiller and lower the centreboard.

Then, having decided in which direction he will pay off, he should pull the tiller up to what will be the **windward** side (the side *nearest* the wind), and the crewman should pull hard on the bow to draw the boat out into deeper water. As the boat moves past him, the crewman should get aboard quickly, always on the windward side so that the wind, now pressing on the sails, will help to balance his weight as soon as he comes in over the side. As soon as he is aboard, his first job is to haul on the jib sheet on the **leeward** side (the side *away from* the wind) so that the sail fills with wind and the boat gathers way: the helmsman can gradually haul on the mainsheet to make the mainsail draw.

What a place to capsize — right on the line and only seconds before the start of a heat of the National 4.87m Fireball championship. Left and right foreground are a flag and the mast of the official launch.

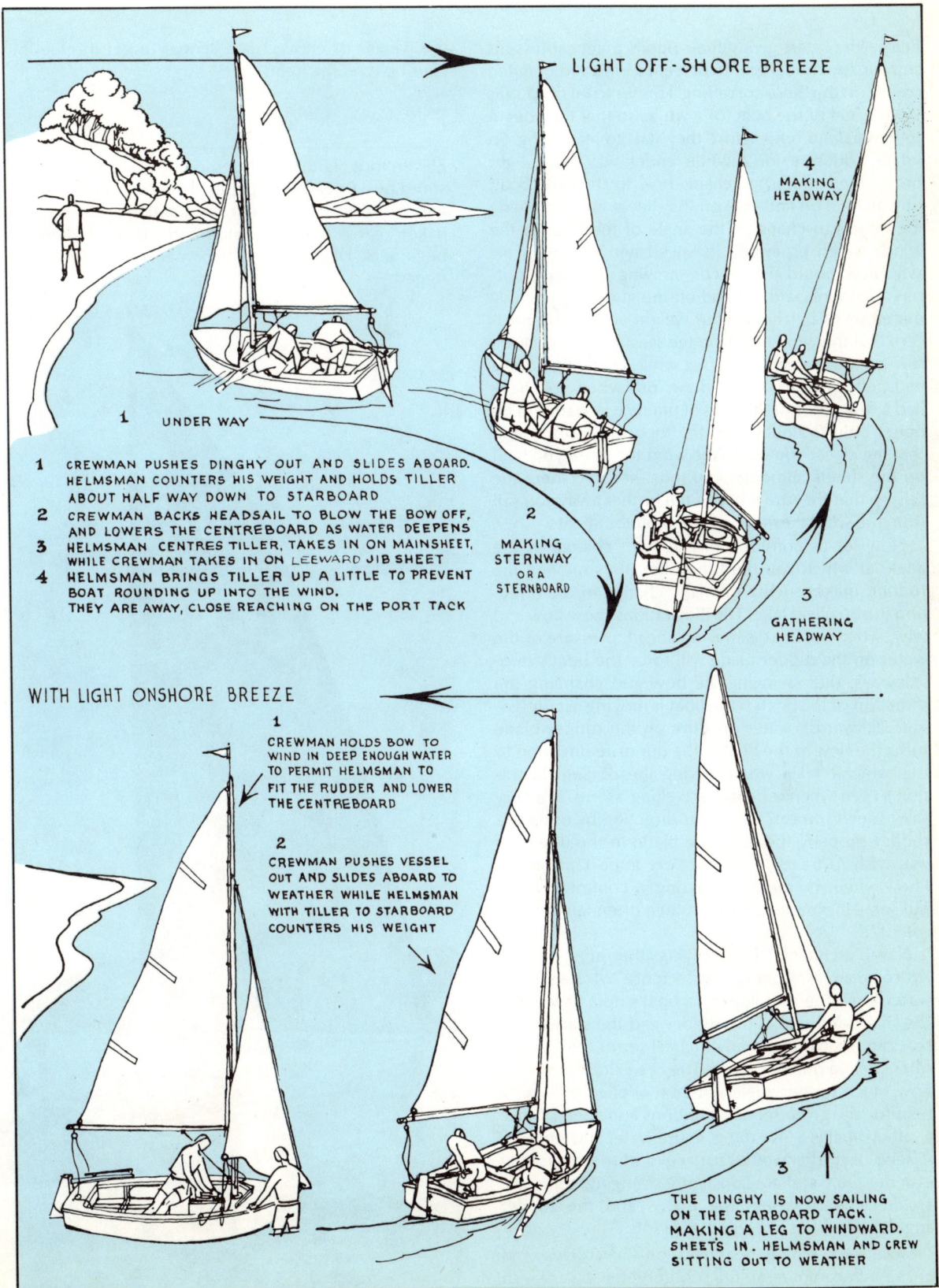

# LESSON 10
# Effect of rudder

Before they start giving their pupils practical lessons some instructors prefer to present a long and detailed course on the theory of sailing. I prefer to let my pupils get the feel of the boat for a while, so that they begin to understand *how* before they start to learn *why*. So let us continue for a while under way (in a light breeze, remember) practising how to steer the boat, how to haul on and ease off the sheets, and observing the effects of changing the angle of the boat to the wind: watch especially its speed and the set of its sails. You should also practise moving your body outboard and inboard, on and off the gunwale, to study the effect of balancing your weight against the pressure that the wind exerts on the sails. You may have a few anxious moments at first while changing course and getting your sails to draw, but when you have had a few hours of this sort of practice you should be better able to understand the theory. Keep in mind that the closer you sail to the wind the more you haul on the sheets (although you must not oversheet the sails so that they are flat) and the further away you sail from the wind the more you ease off the sheets.

Now let us consider why a slight change in the angle at which you hold the tiller, thus moving the rudder, makes such a dramatic change in the direction the boat will take. The illustrations show how and why, when the boat is moving ahead, pressure of the water on the rudder blade will force the boat's stern sideways, thus swinging the bow and changing the direction of the boat. If the boat is moving astern (going backwards), water pressure on the rudder blade turns the bow of the boat in the opposite direction to that which it takes when moving ahead. (See illustration.) Even when a boat is travelling astern at a very slow speed you can change its direction by using the rudder properly (pointing the blade in the direction you wish to travel). This is a very important fact to know when you are manoeuvring in confined waters but some inexperienced yachtsmen often fail to make use of it.

Naval architects, by applying the principles of hydrodynamics (simply, the science of measuring water forces) to the shape of a boat's hull, its weight, the shape and size of the rudder and the state of the sea, can resolve into mathematical terms these water forces acting on the rudder. They can show *in theory* how much rudder angle must be applied to steer a boat for any given set of conditions and speed. Since a sailing boat is a 'live thing' in the water and since, as it heels over, the 'wetted surface' and *the shape* that is under the water are constantly changing, the naval architects must assess the forces and the rudder angles in the form of a complex graph.

Since every type of boat has a different shape, and because the amount of hull submerged will vary with the weight of crew, it is essential to get the feel of *your* boat on the helm.

Eleven foot (3.35m) Mirror dinghies, originally sponsored by a British newspaper, are simply constructed and most are home-built by amateurs. Their spinnaker gear is uncomplicated and easily handled by beginners. Like Herons, their mainsails are gunter-rigged.

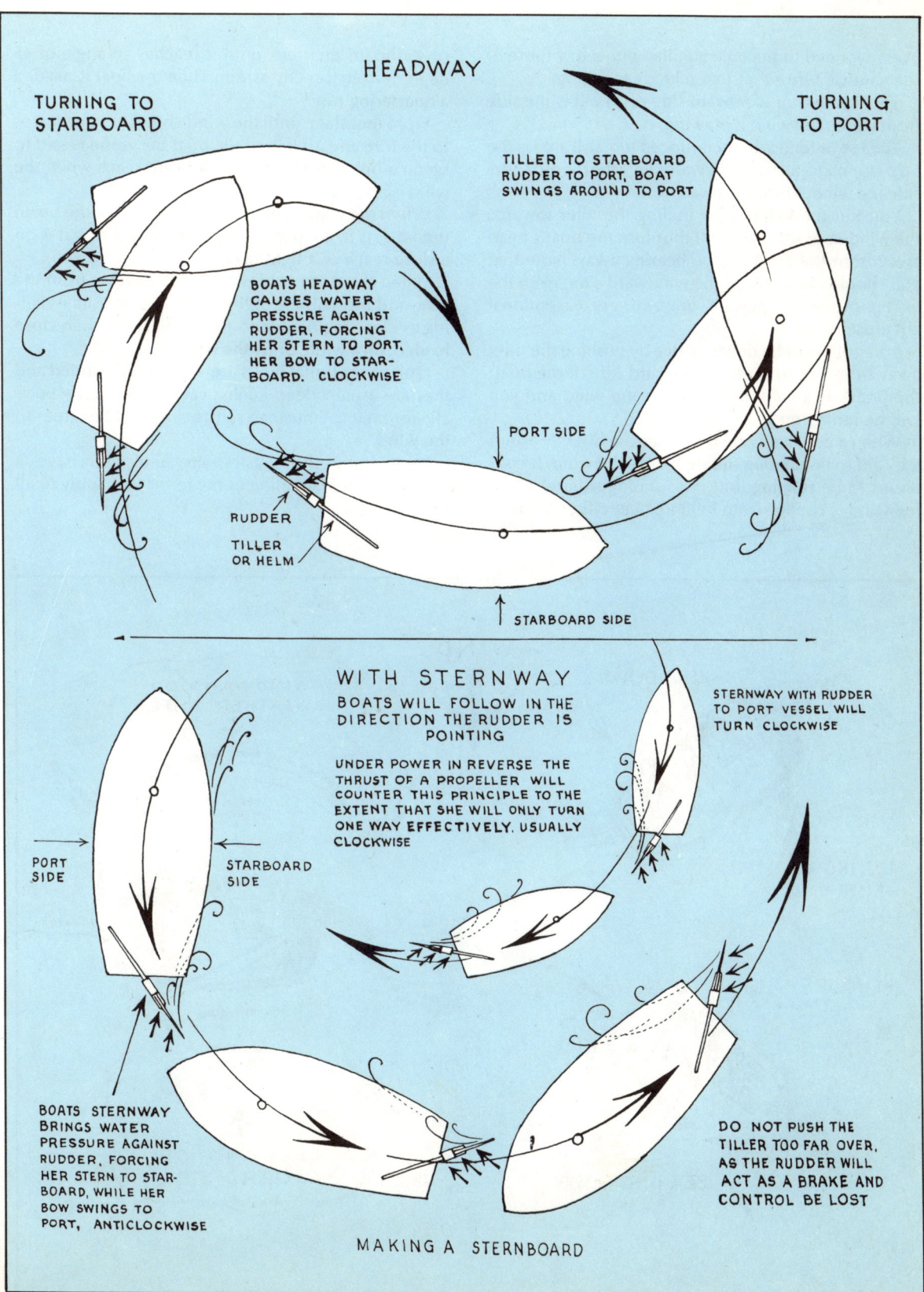

# LESSON 11
## Nautical terms

We now need to become familiar with a few more of the nautical terms that are exclusive to sailing.

The **weather** or **windward** side of a boat is the side from which the wind is blowing.

The **lee** or **leeward** (pronounced loo'ard) side is the side opposite to the windward; in other words, the side the wind is blowing away from.

You put the **helm up** by pulling the tiller towards the windward side: you will thus turn the boat's head away from the wind and be **bearing away**. Note that you should always sit on the windward side; even the expert moves to leeward only in very exceptional circumstances.

You put the **helm down** or **alee** by pushing the tiller away from you towards the leeward side of the boat: the boat's head will turn towards the wind and you will be **luffing up**.

When a boat has wind blowing from directly astern it is said to be **running square** before the wind. It continues to be **running** (but not running square) while the wind is coming from behind, over either the port or starboard quarters, until it reaches an angle of 45 degrees from directly astern. Then the boat is making a **quartering run**.

From that stage until the wind comes at right angles to the fore and aft line of the boat the vessel is said to be on a **broad reach**. It is on a beam **reach** when the wind is at right angles to the bow.

When the wind is blowing from ahead of the beam until it gets to 45 degrees from the bow the boat is on a **close reach** or a **tight reach**.

When the wind is blowing at 45 degrees from the bow and the sails are still full the boat is usually sailing as close as possible to the wind. She is then **close hauled**, **on a wind**, or **by the wind**.

Only exceptional boats are very **closed winded** and they are usually deep-keeled yachts designed especially for racing. Some can sail as close as 32 degrees to the wind.

Now study the illustrations until you have a thorough understanding of the terms that apply to all these angles.

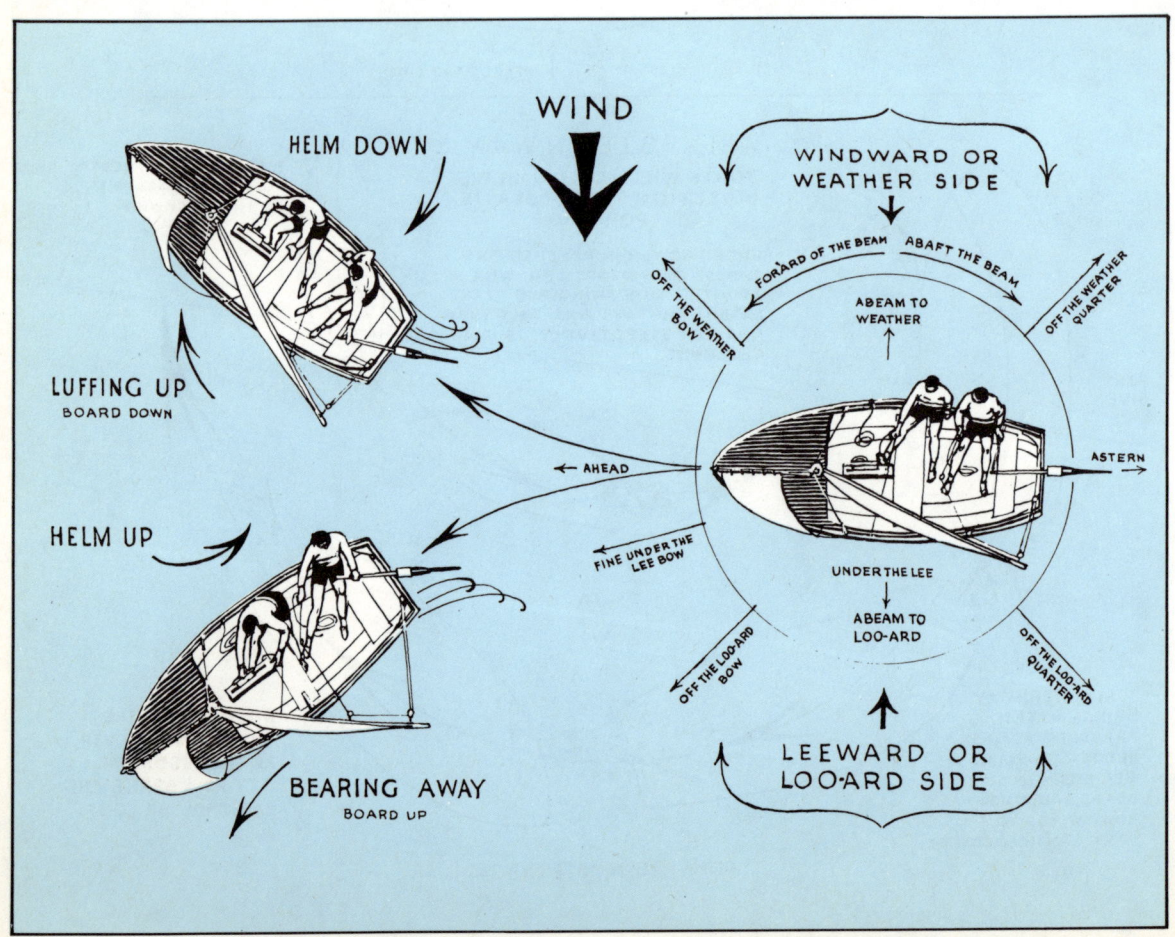

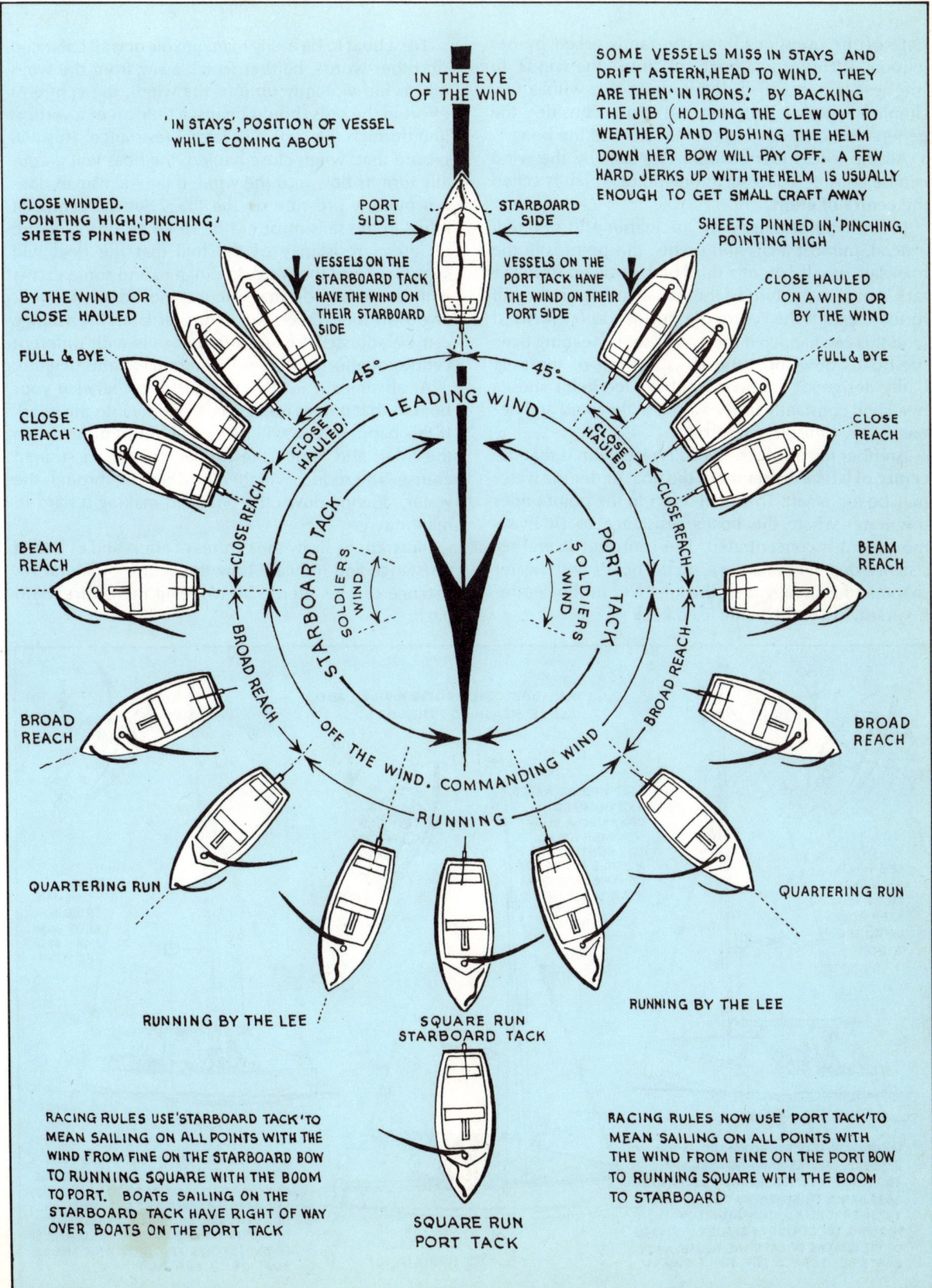

# LESSON 12
## Centre of effort

One of the questions I am constantly asked by beginners is 'How can a boat sail "into" the wind?' In the next lesson I shall demonstrate this with a few simple diagrams. But first we must consider the general forces exerted upon the sails and the boat.

All the forces exerted upon the sails by the wind can be considered to act at one point which is called the **centre of effort**.

In the type of dinghy we are learning to sail and, indeed, in most boats and yachts, this point is in the mainsail, usually about a third of the way up from the tack and about a third of the way across from the luff to the leech. If the centre of effort is too far forward (and this can happen if the mast is set up leaning over the boat's bows or if the jib is too big or the sails badly designed) the boat will have **lee helm** and its head will constantly turn away from the wind and become very difficult to control.

Another factor which can cause lee helm is that the **centre of lateral resistance** of the boat under the water may be too far aft. This term refers to the point under the water where the boat's resistance to sideways movement is concentrated. The centre of lateral resistance depends, of course, on the boat's underwater shape and is usually near the keel and in the centreboard or, in a yacht, in the fixed keel.

For a boat to be easily manageable or well balanced (in other words, neither to fall away from the wind nor to luff violently up into the wind), the centre of effort in the sails should be just a little aft of a vertical line through the centre of lateral resistance. This will ensure that, when close hauled, the boat will gradually turn its bow into the wind, if the helmsman does not put any pressure on the tiller. But the centre of effort in the sails must not be so far aft of the centre of lateral resistance of the hull that the boat will swoop up into the wind. In dinghies and some yachts with centreboards that can be moved to different angles in their cases, the centre of lateral resistance can be adjusted to suit different sails with different centres of effort, and to suit different weights of wind.

At all times it is advisable to try to balance your boat so that it does not 'gripe' violently into the wind. If this happens you will be forced to put pressure on the tiller, and hence the rudder, to steer a straight course. The rudder will then be dragging through the water, slowing down the boat and making it hard to manoeuvre.

Illustrations show the centres of effort and of lateral resistance and indicate how the centre of lateral resistance can be altered by swinging the centreboard back.

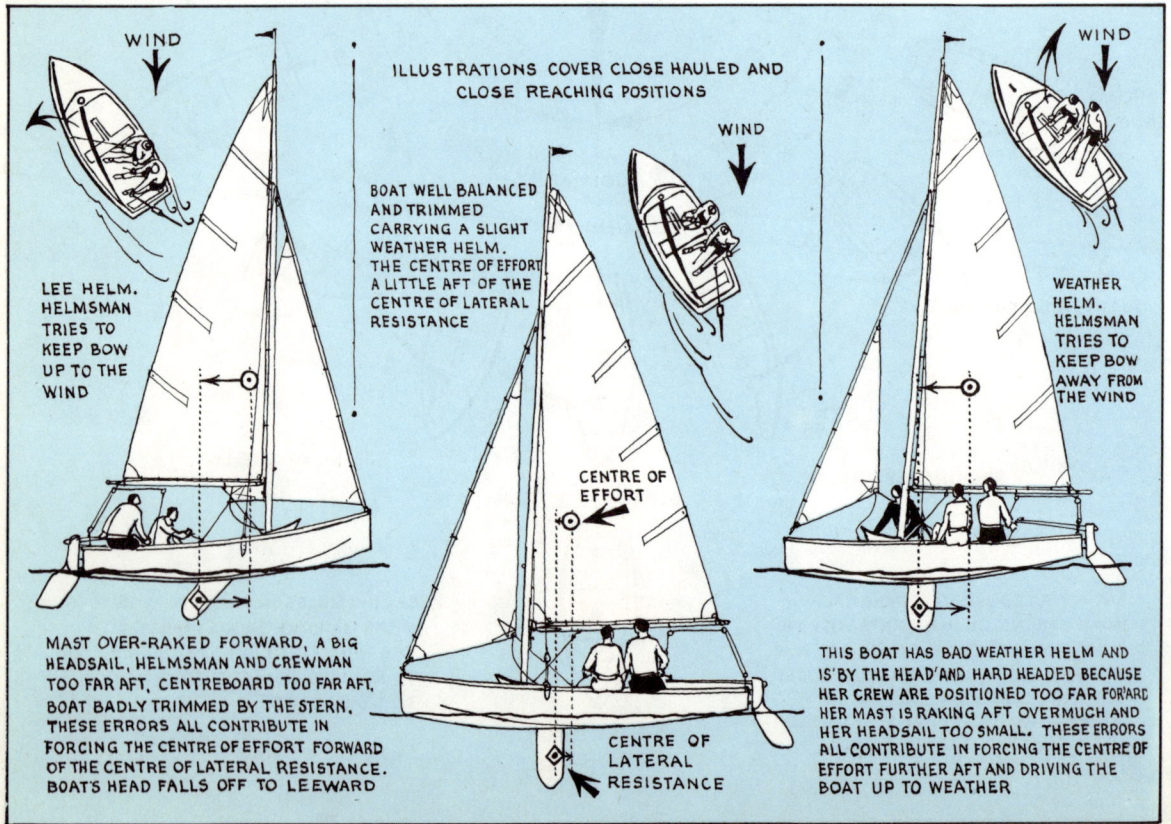

# LESSON 13
# Wind forces

In the illustrations the theoretical wind forces exerted on the sails are shown for three different points of sailing.

In the first illustration the wind is shown coming from ahead when the boat is close-hauled on a port tack, that is, with the wind coming over the port side at 45 degrees from the bow. The arrow labelled A shows the direction of the wind as it blows into the mainsail. (The only reason we have not shown the jib in this illustration is to avoid complicating the diagram.) The wind pressure exerts force shown by the line B which is at right angles to the surface of the sail. Having extended the line B as the diagonal of a parallelogram we can then resolve the force into two parts. The directions of these forces are shown by the base line, labelled C, and the perpendicular line, labelled D. In addition, the lengths of these lines show approximately the relative magnitudes of the forces with the wind blowing at about 45 degrees from the bow.

The parallelogram is known as the **parallelogram of forces**. The perpendicular D is the **headway** the boat will make when sailing close-hauled and the base line C is the **leeway**. You can see from the illustration that on this point of sailing there is in theory a much greater tendency for the boat to make leeway than headway. However, the underwater body shape of a properly designed sailing boat and the use of the centreboard (or, in the case of a yacht, a fixed keel) help to reduce the leeway.

In the next illustration, with the wind blowing from abeam, the boat is sailing on a beam reach and, with the force line B still at right angles to the surface of the sail, you can see that there is less tendency to make leeway and more tendency to make headway.

In the third illustration, with the wind blowing over the port quarter, headway increases still more in proportion to leeway.

You must understand that these are greatly simplified explanations of the forces that interact to make a boat progress through the water under sail. Wind tunnel tests and studies of aerodynamics show that it is the suction on the leeward side of the sails—a vacuum effect created by the flow of wind on to the windward sides and along and around their curved shapes—that generates the forces. These are complex theories which, for all practical purposes, it is not necessary to consider, so long as we know how to control the forces and use them to the advantage of our boat.

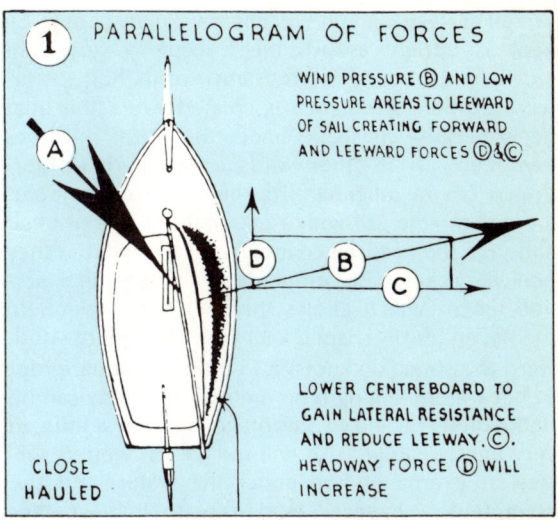

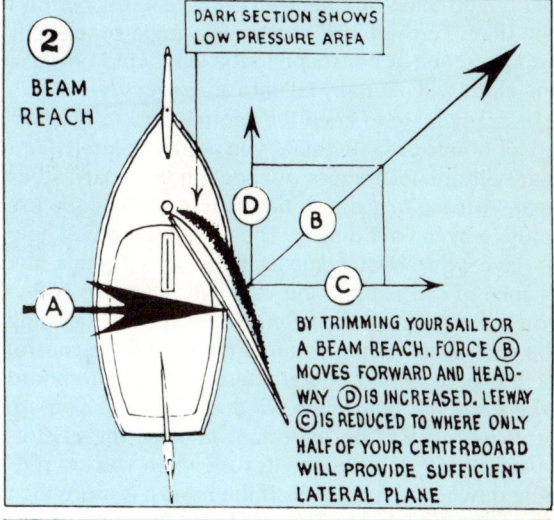

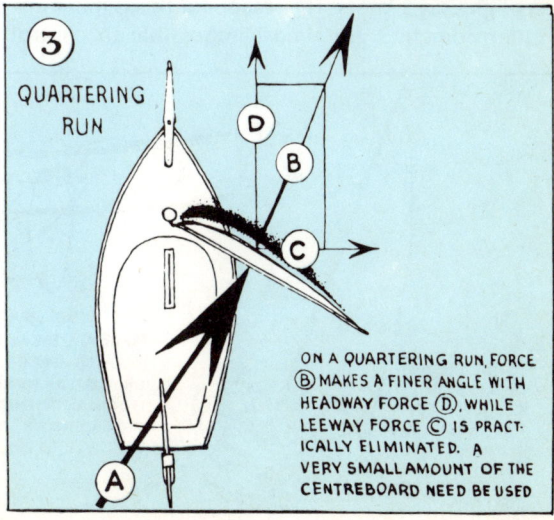

# LESSON 14
# Resistance and balance

To sail at its maximum efficiency a dinghy should be kept as upright as possible (except in very light weather) to reduce the resistance of its hull to forward motion. Resistance is created when the boat heels because its shape under the water becomes asymmetrical—in other words, not properly proportioned. On the other hand, the hulls of most keelboats are designed to sail with a reasonable angle of heel; although their resistance increases somewhat as they heel, they gain some compensatory increase in waterline length which allows them to travel faster. In theory, an ideally shaped keel yacht can sail to windward at a speed (in knots) 2.43 times the square root of her waterline length (in metres). A dinghy can be deliberately heeled to advantage, but only a little, in very light weather. This will reduce its 'wetted surface' (the area of hull under the water) and the asymmetrical shape will tend to create slight weather helm, and allow the helmsman to 'feel' his boat on the tiller. Furthermore, the heeled angle of the sails will present a better shape to the light wind because the cloth will naturally fall into an even curve.

It is advisable to keep the centreboard fully down on all points of sailing until you are completely familiar with the techniques of handling the boat and its gear—for the first dozen times, at least, that you are under way in your dinghy. The centreboard will help to give your boat some stability and reduce the chance of capsizing in the very light winds to which you must restrict your sailing while you are learning the rudiments. When you feel that you have control of the boat, you can start raising the centreboard when running before the wind. (As soon as you are proficient, it will be important to raise the centreboard almost right up into its case when you are running downwind, especially if the breeze is more than very light, say 5 knots. The reason for this is that most modern dinghies are almost impossible to control square before the wind when their centreboards are right down. Any slight change in the boat's course will cause the centreboard to grip the water and the craft will swing violently out of control).

By retracting the centreboard almost completely when running downwind you will not only make the boat more controllable, but also increase its speed by reducing resistance. With the sheets eased, the centre of effort will have moved aft of its normal on-a-wind position. To compensate for this, the helmsman and crewman should move their weight slightly further aft than when on a beam reach, but not so far that the transom buries and causes drag.

When sailing to windward one should remember that the boat will have its greatest tendency to make leeway, so the centreboard should be fully lowered to help counteract this effect. Since the centre of effort in the sails will be closest to the mast when on a wind, the crewman and helmsman should keep their weight as far forward in the boat as is necessary to keep the bows from lifting. This will also help to align, as nearly as possible, the centre of lateral resistance below the centre of effort.

With the sails eased off for a reach, and the centre of effort thus further aft, the helmsman and crew should move aft of their positions on a wind. The centreboard can then be partly lifted to reduce resistance and also to bring the centre of lateral resistance further aft.

None of these adjustments can be specifically determined for all types of boats. They will depend on the class of boat you are sailing, the rig, and the combined weight of the helmsman and crewman, as well as the wind and sea conditions. Correct adjustments will reduce the amount of pressure you have to exert on the tiller to steer a straight course; by constant practice and systematic assessment of your boat's performance, you will learn to balance her well.

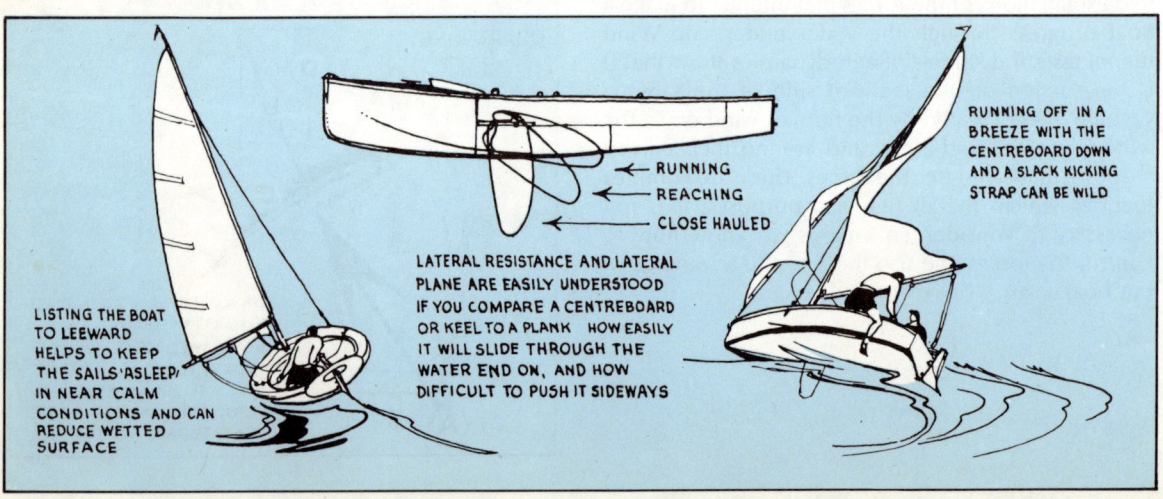

# LESSON 15
# Tacking

You will remember that the closest angle you can hope to sail to the wind in a dinghy is 45 degrees, and that does not take into account the leeway your boat will make 'over the ground'. Thus, to get from one point to another with the wind blowing against you, it will be necessary to sail a zigzag course, first on one tack, with the wind blowing over one side of your bow, and then on another tack, with the wind blowing over the opposite side.

To change from one tack to another you should (from your position on the windward side of the boat) push the tiller away from you so that the boat's bow first comes up directly into the wind then pays off at a little more than 90 degrees from your previous course. At the moment the luff of the jib starts to shudder, as the boat comes up into the wind, your crewman must be ready to let go the jib sheet completely and then haul on the opposite (leeward) jib sheet. At the same time both you, as helmsman, and your crewman must move across the boat to what will *now* be the windward side. You are now on a new tack, called either **port tack** or **starboard tack**, after the side of the boat from which the wind is now blowing. The whole operation is called **going about** or **tacking**.

Here are some points to watch. Don't over-helm your boat by pushing the tiller down suddenly or more than is necessary to make the boat swing smoothly from one tack to another: if you do, the boat is likely to react so violently that you may not have time to get across to the windward side and balance her with your weight. You might even capsize. At best, depending on the weight of wind, she will lose ground and be sailing too low (far away from the wind) on her new course.

Be sure you warn your crewman of the manoeuvre by calling 'Stand by to go about', or 'Ready about'. Realise that if the crewman fails to let go the 'old' jib sheet (which will be on the windward side on the new tack) the boat's bows will swing violently across the wind and the jib, filled with wind across the bows, may 'pin' them down and cause a capsize.

If you and your crewman perform the operation correctly the boat should gather way smoothly on the new tack without losing speed or distance.

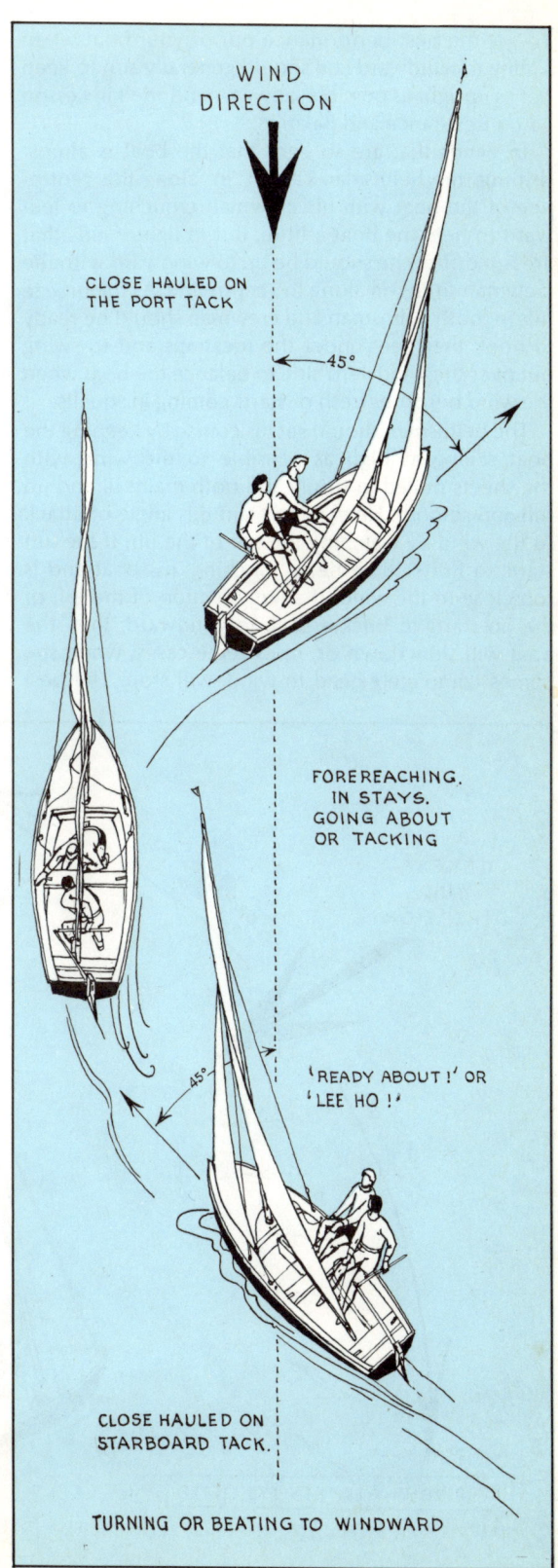

TURNING OR BEATING TO WINDWARD

# LESSON 16
## On a wind

To get the best performance out of your boat when sailing to windward you should generally aim to keep her as upright as possible, as was mentioned in Lesson 14 on Resistance and Balance.

In winds that are so light that the boat is almost drifting, the helmsman can sit 'in' along the centreline of the boat with his crewman crouching to leeward to heel the boat a little. But in light winds that are not drifters he should be up to windward with the crewman sitting-in along the centreline. As the breeze fills in, both helmsman and crewman should be ready to hook their feet under the toestraps and to swing out over the windward side to balance the boat when the wind becomes fresh or starts coming in squalls.

The helmsman should set his course by keeping the boat sailing as high as possible to the wind with the sheets pulled in firmly and both mainsail and jib full and smooth. He can maintain this angle of attack to the wind by watching the luff of the jib. If the luff starts to flutter then he is 'pinching' his boat and is too close to the wind. If a large section of the luff of the jib starts to buckle back to windward, then the boat will slow down or, in extreme cases, when she comes completely head to wind, will stop. The best way to get your boat sailing efficiently on a wind is to bring it up to a point when the luff begins to quiver, then bear away just enough to make it smooth.

When your jib is drawing properly on a wind the mainsail can be gradually eased until its luff begins to 'backwind'. Then, provided the breeze is light to moderate, the mainsheet should be hauled in just enough to smooth out the buckle in the luff.

You will rarely be able to set a course and stay rigidly on it because the wind seldom blows exactly from the one point. It changes constantly and irregularly in direction and strength, demanding that the helmsman constantly adjust his course to suit the prevailing direction of the wind. With experience you will be able to anticipate these wind shifts and especially their increase in strength by watching for a darkening, ruffled patch on the surface of the water about two hundred yards ahead and to windward of your boat's bow. These are called 'darkies'. After lots of practice you will also be able to detect changes in the direction of light winds by observing the way that small, fan-shaped ripples, a few yards to windward of your bow, change their course.

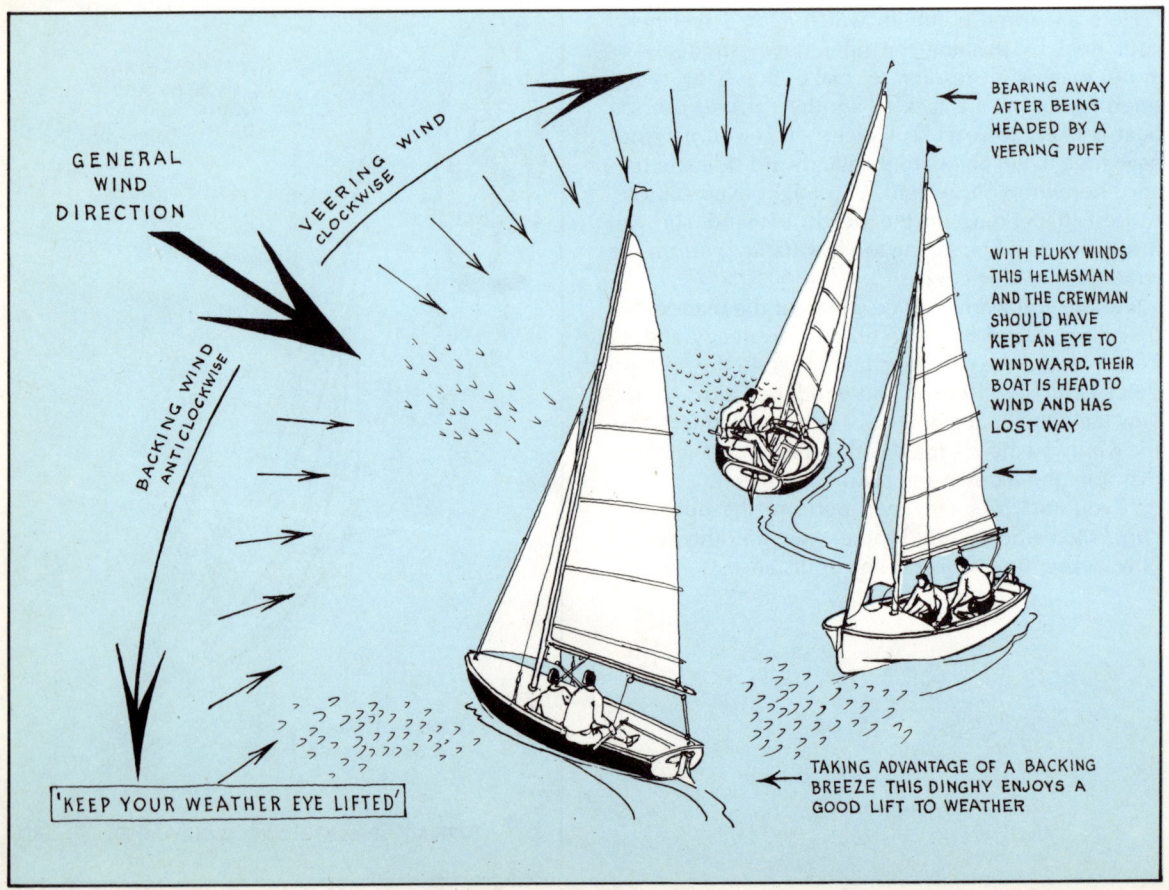

# LESSON 17
# Fresh conditions

When sailing on a wind in fresh winds or squally conditions it is not necessary to keep the luff of the mainsail full all the time to maintain speed. In fact, even when the helmsman and crewman are swinging out over the side to keep the boat upright, it will often be necessary to ease off the mainsheet and release some of the excess pressure in the mainsail. Thus, since the mainsheet and the jib sheet of a dinghy may need to be instantly released, neither should be cleated down. The sheets can, however, be led through ready-release cam cleats so long as the tail of each sheet is held in one hand (the crewman usually on the jib and the helmsman on the mainsheet)—then a quick flick will let them run freely.

To prevent the boat heeling too much in squalls the helmsman can luff and spill some wind out of both sails or ease the mainsheet, or do both. As a general rule the jib should not be eased except to prevent a capsize. The reason for keeping the jib on is to maintain the boat's forward movement and thus give her steerage way. If you lose steerage way in a hard breeze the boat will be almost unmanageable and in danger of capsize as soon as a gust hits her.

Should you find the wind altogether too strong for you to manage the boat under full sail, remember that you can lower the mainsail and run before the wind under jib. Before you attempt to lower the mainsail be sure to ease the mainsheet and to bring the boat well up to the wind with the jib luffing, although still drawing a little. It is better to keep on some steerage way, so do not put the boat dead into the wind for the manoeuvre, otherwise you will have no control when you are lowering the mainsail and may capsize. Be sure that your crewman is ready to release the main halyard and check that it will run freely as you come up to the wind so that the sail will lower quickly. Then bear away on the same tack and ease your jib well off as you come on to a broad reach; gather in the mainsail and furl it into as tight a roll as you can manage, to stop the wind getting into it.

If your course is then running you into danger you should round up to the wind again and lower your jib, too. Even with both sails lowered and furled you will make some progress downwind in a high wind but this procedure will give you a much greater chance of getting safely ashore or of being rescued.

As a general principle, until you are quite expert it is foolish to attempt sailing in a dinghy when winds of more than twenty knots are likely, so always check the official weather bureau forecast for your area before you rig your boat.

IF THE WIND IS TOO HEAVY FOR YOU, LOWER THE MAIN AND SCUD OFF UNDER JIB OR BARE POLES TO A PREDETERMINED BEACH OR LANDING PLACE TO LEEWARD UNDER A LEE IF POSSIBLE

LUFF THROUGH THE STRONG GUSTS AND WHEN NECESSARY SPILL SOME WIND FROM THE SAILS BY EASING THE SHEETS. KEEP GOOD WAY ON THE VESSEL BY HARDENING IN ON THE SHEETS AS SOON AS THE GUST EASES

# LESSON 18
# Gybing

A beam reach, with the sheets well off so that the sails are just nicely full, is a pleasant point of sailing and probably the easiest. It gives maximum control because one may easily change course either side of the general track one is steering—by hauling on the sheets one may come up 45 degrees to the on-a-wind position, or by easing the sheets right away one may swing down 90 degrees until the wind is directly astern and the boom is almost at right angles to the boat.

When you are running square downwind, even in a moderate breeze, it is a safe practice not to let your sheets so far off that the boom rubs against the leeward shroud. Should you do this, the boom will be chafed and a fold may be formed in the mainsail which can become pinched between the boom and the shroud, causing fraying.

While the wind is directly astern it is also important for helmsman and crewman to be on the alert for a sudden shift in its direction bringing it round the back of the mainsail, in other words, blowing from the same side as the boom. Then the boat will be running **by the lee.** This is not really catastrophic and, in certain conditions—say because of the position of other boats or of the shoreline—it may be necessary to run by the lee for short periods. Generally, though, beginners should avoid running by the lee, because the angle of the sail to the wind tends to make the boat roll and lose speed. Furthermore, there is always the chance of the helmsman losing control under these conditions, since a momentary change of the boat's course to leeward can cause an involuntary gybe.

**Gybe** is the name given to the operation when the boat turns so that the wind crosses the stern and causes the sails to change sides.

An involuntary gybe in a hard wind can slam the boom across so violently that it may break the shroud it hits, dismast the boat or, if the crew does not move across quickly enough to balance it, cause a capsize. By watching the boat's burgee or by noting that the jib is tending to swing across and fill on the windward side or that the boom is tending to lift excessively you may see that you are running by the lee. If so, you can prevent a gybe by pushing the tiller very slightly towards the boom; this will bring the wind directly astern again or, if you keep the tiller down, bring the wind over your windward quarter.

Gybing under control, however, is quite a regular and necessary part of sailing when changing course downwind, and should be practised in very light conditions 'all standing'. To do this, merely bring the breeze square astern and then pull the tiller a little towards you (away from the boom). Your crewman can then swing the boom over to the opposite side. Each of you should also, at the same time, be ready to change your positions to balance the boat; you, as helmsman, having moved to the windward side, must immediately pull away on to the new course so that you don't round up into the wind. Then both of you can adjust your sheets to suit the new angle of the breeze. When you perform this manoeuvre smoothly you will find that the boat will not roll or lose much speed.

Until you are really experienced in light to moderate winds, do not attempt such an all-standing gybe in a fresh breeze. You will find that by gripping all parts of your mainsheet you can swing the boom across as you bring your tiller towards you to change course. You must also co-ordinate the operation with your transfer of position across the boat to the new windward side.

In a keelboat you can perform a controlled gybe from any angle of sailing in moderate to fresh conditions by hauling in your sheets, altering course to bring the breeze astern then, as it comes alee (by the lee) and the sails swing across, easing out the sheets. But this is rarely possible in a dinghy because when you start to haul in the mainsheet the dinghy will swing up into the wind and resist the thrust of the rudder blade to turn the boat's head away. If you do succeed in gybing a dinghy with the mainsheet hauled in, in a hard wind there is also the danger of getting out of control, spinning up into the wind, or capsizing before you can ease off the mainsail to keep the boat properly on a downwind course.

Therefore, in hard winds, until you have lots of experience, it is better to tack than to gybe. To do this, starting with the wind square astern, it is essential to keep the boat under way at all times. Do not just shove the tiller down with the sheets free and expect the boat to swing all the way through 360 degrees without faltering. Instead, first lower the centreboard right down, then haul on the sheets until you are properly on a wind and tack in the orthodox way. When you are on the new tack, ease away the sheets until you are on the course you need.

When running square or almost square you will find that your jib is almost useless because it is largely blanketed by the mainsail and does not present its surface to the wind. However, you can make the jib effective by goose-winging it, i.e. by booming it out on the windward side (the opposite side to the main boom) with a whisker pole. This whisker pole may be of wood or aluminium tube: its diameter need be only about half that of the main boom, and its length about twice the beam of the boat at the mast, according to the size of the jib your boat carries. It has a clip on one end to attach it to a fitting on the mast and a clip or a rounded metal spike on the other end.

To set the whisker pole, you first pull the jib over to

the windward side and fit the spiked end (or the clip) to the jib clew shackle. Then you push the pole forward and outward, attach the inner end to the mast and haul on the windward jib sheet to bring the pole at right angles to the boat to make the jib fill with wind. With a little practice you will find exactly the right angle at which to set the pole and the jib and thus considerably increase your speed downwind. Remember it is best to unship and stow your whisker pole before you attempt to gybe.

Some boats and yachts, such as the Heron and International Star class, which are restricted to mainsail and jib for downwind running and are not allowed to carry spinnakers (which we shall discuss later), goose-wing their jibs to great effect.

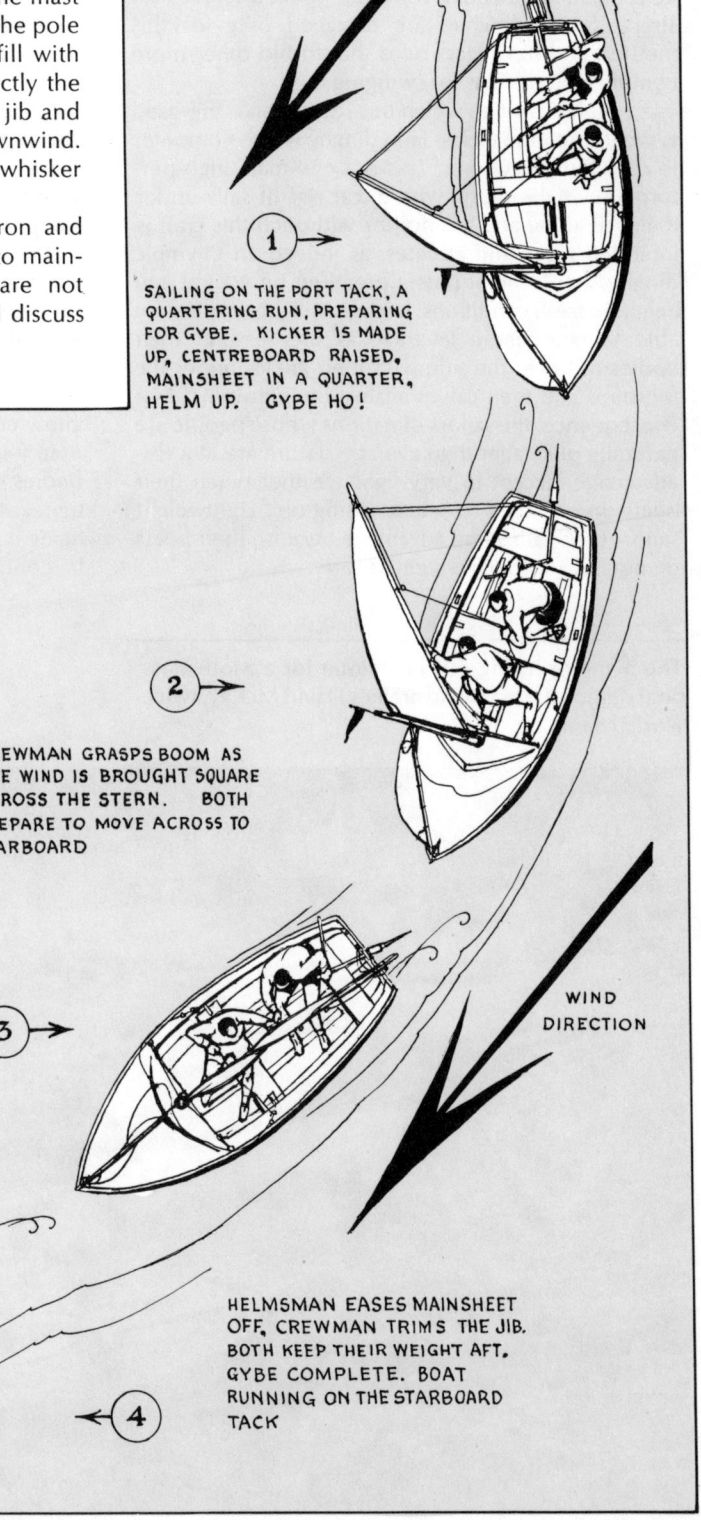

# LESSON 19
# Balancing the boat

So far we have considered only the simple and obvious method of leaning bodily over the side to help balance our boat, with feet hooked under toestraps. Some dinghies are designed only for this method and have class rules that forbid other more complicated devices for swinging out.

A notable craft on which this restriction is imposed is the international class Finn dinghy which competes in the Olympic Games. This is a one-man, high-performance 4.49 metre, with a 'cat rig' (it sails under mainsail alone and has no jib). Although this craft is intended for skilful athletes, as indeed an Olympic dinghy should be, it puts a premium on weight and height in fresh conditions, because tall, heavy men are able to exert more leverage as they extend their bodies out over the side with their ankles under the toestraps and their calves against the gunwales. As a consequence, the sailors of nations whose people are naturally of smaller than average stature are at a disadvantage, except in very light weather when their boats do not need so much 'sitting up'. Lightweight sailors then gain some advantage because their boats do not have so much weight to carry.

Because of such potential inequalities between people of different physique, the trend during recent years has been to rig mechanical devices on racing dinghies so that even lightweight sailors can get far enough out over the sides to balance their boats in heavy weather. Some classes have incorporated into their designs sliding planks (attached to the decks through brackets) which allow crewmen to lie out on them full length to windward; others have complicated handstraps and foot sockets so that crews and skippers can lean outboard.

The most successful development has been a light trapeze harness fitting under the buttocks and around the hips and attached with ready-release clips to special wires rigged either side of the mast. (More advanced models fit around the back and over the shoulders as well, to give full body support.) These allow crewmen and, in some classes of boats helmsmen too, to stand on the gunwales and extend their bodies out over the water almost horizontally. Thus trapezes provide tremendous leverage, and have made it possible for lightweight crews and helmsmen to control boats which in fresh winds would pre-

The acme of hiking out technique for a Moth class boat demonstrated by Australia's David McKay, twice world champion.

viously have been beyond them. In some classes of boats, notably those which used to depend on large crews leaning over the side to keep them upright, trapezes have halved the number of men needed aboard.

In lulls between gusts of wind trapezemen can bring their weight inboard merely by bending their knees or can swing right back into the body of the boat by lifting their feet. In addition, the ready-release clips on the harnesses allow them to make quick switches from side to side when the boats are tacking or gybing.

As in every other phase of this fascinating sport, one does not learn to become a competent trapeze-man without constant practice.

## Rules of the Road

At this stage, before we proceed with more advanced aspects of sailing, it is important to know some of your responsibilities on the water. There must be rules for traffic afloat just as there are for traffic on the roads. Only by meticulous observance of these rules can you expect to move from place to place in safety and comfort. The thirty-eight nautical Rules of the Road are called Regulations for Preventing Collisions at Sea. They are international and apply to all types of vessels.

Four main rules govern the behaviour of sailing craft. In simplified terms these are:

**1** Boats on a port tack (with the wind on the port side) must give way to boats on a starboard tack (with the wind on the starboard side). It does not make any difference if one is on a wind and the other is running free.

**2** When two or more boats are on the same tack (with the wind coming over the same side) each boat that is to windward (closer to the wind) of another must keep clear of the boat that is to leeward (further away from the wind).

**3** Overtaking boats must keep clear of the boats they are overtaking (whether under sail or power). A boat that is catching up on another is an overtaking boat until she has established an overlap on the other; that is, until a part of her bow (or bowsprit) is ahead of a part of the stern of the boat she is approaching.

**4** Power boats must give way to sailing boats but a sailing boat must not hinder a power boat in a narrow channel or in any other circumstance which makes it difficult for the power boat to manoeuvre.

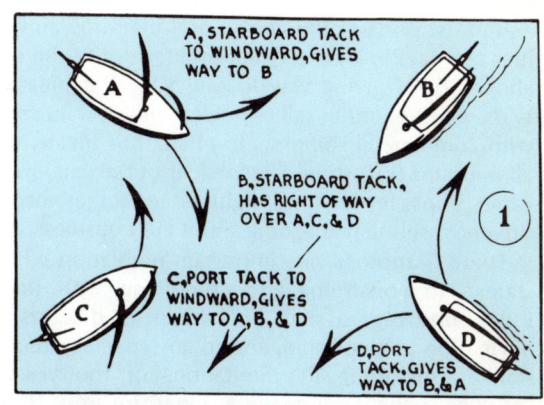

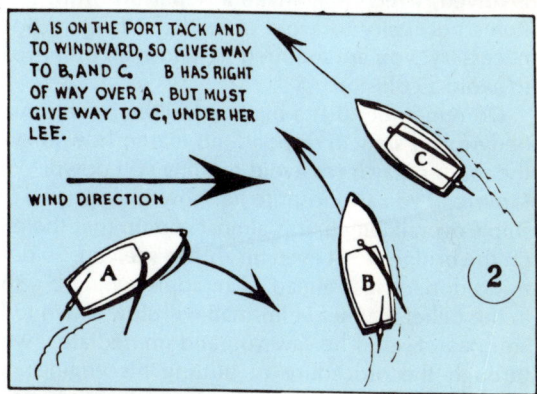

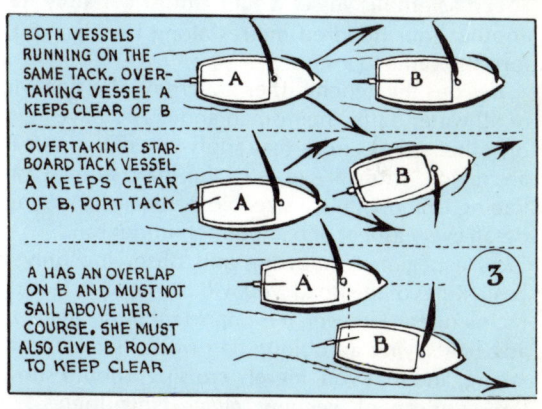

In most ports of the world local maritime authorities also lay down a very important rider to the rule about power giving way to sail, viz., that pleasure craft, whether under sail or power, must not interfere with commercial shipping. In effect, this means that all pleasure craft should keep clear of passenger and cargo ships, ferries, tugs, lighters and other motor-driven vessels that are going about their business.

**There is another very important regulation which states:** 'In construing and complying with these Rules, due regard shall be had to all dangers of navigation and collision, and to any special circumstances, including the limitations of the vessels involved, which may make a departure from these Rules necessary to avoid immediate danger.' So, if necessary, you are required to ignore all other rules to avoid a collision.

Do remember that a big ship will be hard to manoeuvre and slow to respond, no matter how anxious the master may be to avoid running you down. What is more, if you are closer to her bows than a third of a ship's overall length, it is almost certain that the men on the bridge won't even be able to see you. So don't try to dodge close ahead of an approaching big ship in the belief that her helmsman will slow down to let you pass. Even if he saw you and immediately went through the procedure of putting his engines full speed astern his vessel would almost certainly travel another four hundred metres along her course before she came to a stop.

Besides the general rules governing the behaviour of all water traffic, helmsmen and crews have agreed on other special rules that apply to sailing craft that are racing. These are rules of the International Yacht Racing Union, filling a sizeable book and covering in detail every aspect of competition under sail.

As a beginner, knowing and observing only the basic Rules of the Road, you will not need to learn the racing rules. However, it *is* important to be aware that any boat flying an oblong flag from its masthead is racing, and that you, merely cruising, should show it the courtesy of keeping clear. Nevertheless, her oblong flag does not confer any rights on the racing vessel and in the event of a collision the basic Rules of the Road, where they differ from the racing rules, will apply.

When you are thoroughly proficient in handling a boat and ready to join a club to race, you will need to spend a considerable time studying racing rules and attending the club's lectures on this matter.

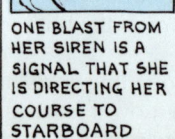

IF YOU ARE NOT RACING AND HAVE RIGHT OF WAY OVER YACHTS THAT ARE RACING, IT IS COURTEOUS TO KEEP CLEAR. SHOW THEM YOUR INTENTION AS EARLY AS POSSIBLE TO AVOID ANY CONFUSION

BIG SHIPS ARE HARD TO MANOEUVRE AT LOW SPEEDS AND HAVE TO KEEP TO SET CHANNELS

THIS VESSEL IS STANDING ON TOO LONG, SHE SHOULD HAVE COME ABOUT EARLIER. HER SKIPPER'S BEHAVIOUR IS LUBBERLY & UNSEAMANLIKE

FERRIES HAVE RIGHT OF WAY AND IN THE NARROW HARBOUR BAYS CANNOT GIVE WAY AND MAINTAIN CONTROL

ONE BLAST FROM HER SIREN IS A SIGNAL THAT SHE IS DIRECTING HER COURSE TO STARBOARD

TWO BLASTS, SHE IS DIRECTING HER COURSE TO PORT

THREE BLASTS, ENGINES GOING ASTERN. THE BECALMED SAIL BOAT COULD HAVE PADDLED CLEAR EARLIER

# LESSON 20
# Rigging a spinnaker

When you have mastered all points of sailing in the earlier lessons, have had experience in all weights of wind and are thoroughly confident about handling your boat, it is time to learn how to set a **spinnaker.** This is essentially an extra sail to increase your speed when off a wind and also helps to balance the weight of wind in the mainsail. Spinnakers were once considered sails to be used only when racing, but nowadays cruising boats carry spinnakers as a matter of course

A spinnaker for a dinghy is made of very light fabric, usually nylon, and is triangular in shape with 'bagginess' in it to catch the wind. It can be 'flat cut' (with least bagginess) for beam and even close reaches or 'full cut' like a parachute for quartering runs or square runs. See illustrations. A flat-cut spinnaker is usually longer on the luff than on the leech, with the foot shorter still; a full-cut parachute spinnaker has luff and leech of the same length but with the foot shorter.

Ideally a spinnaker is hoisted on its own spinnaker halyard, which is rigged through a sheave above the jib halyard and also above the forestay. If the jib has been lowered, the spinnaker can be hoisted on the jib halyard.

The tack of the spinnaker is extended forward or outward from the boat, according to the angle of the breeze, with a spinnaker pole. On most modern dinghies this pole is a hollow tube of aluminium alloy (but it can also be of wood), with a metal clip on the end to fasten into the tack **thimble** (a metal eyelet) of the spinnaker. The inner end of the spinnaker pole is fastened low down to the foreside of the mast with another clip that fits into a metal eye attached to the mast, allowing the pole to swing from side to side and the outer end to rise and fall. On some boats and yachts the inner end of the spinnaker pole may have jaws to fit around the mast or may be sharpened to a blunt cone to fit into a swivelling metal cup or even, in an emergency or on a primitive rig, into a **snotter** (a tight loop) of rope or wire. The best type of spinnaker pole is one with a spring-piston type of 'parrot beak' clip on each end, which fastens by snapping into a ring. Then either end of the pole can be attached to a ring on the foreside of the mast, or clipped into a metal ring or loop of wire on the tack of the sail.

To control the outer end of the spinnaker pole one uses a **brace**—a length of rope in dinghies and small yachts or wire in big yachts and ocean racers. On a simple spinnaker rig this brace can be tied to the outer end of the pole or may have a strong clip that fits into the ring on the tack of the sail, or it may have a ring that fits the parrot beak at the end of the pole. The brace must be led back aft outside all the standing rigging through a lead block placed on the quarter or on a spot further forward, according to the length of the pole and the size of the spinnaker.

To stop the outer end of the spinnaker pole rising excessively or 'skying' when the sail is full of wind, a **foreguy** or **kicker downhaul** of rope (or wire for big yachts) is led down to the foredeck from the end of the pole or from a sling of wire under the pole. A spinnaker **topping lift** of wire or rope coming from about half way up the foreside of the mast to the middle of the spinnaker pole is regularly used to stop the pole falling. Finally, to the clew of the spinnaker there is attached a spinnaker sheet, also brought aft outside all the standing rigging, through a lead block, to control the set of the sail.

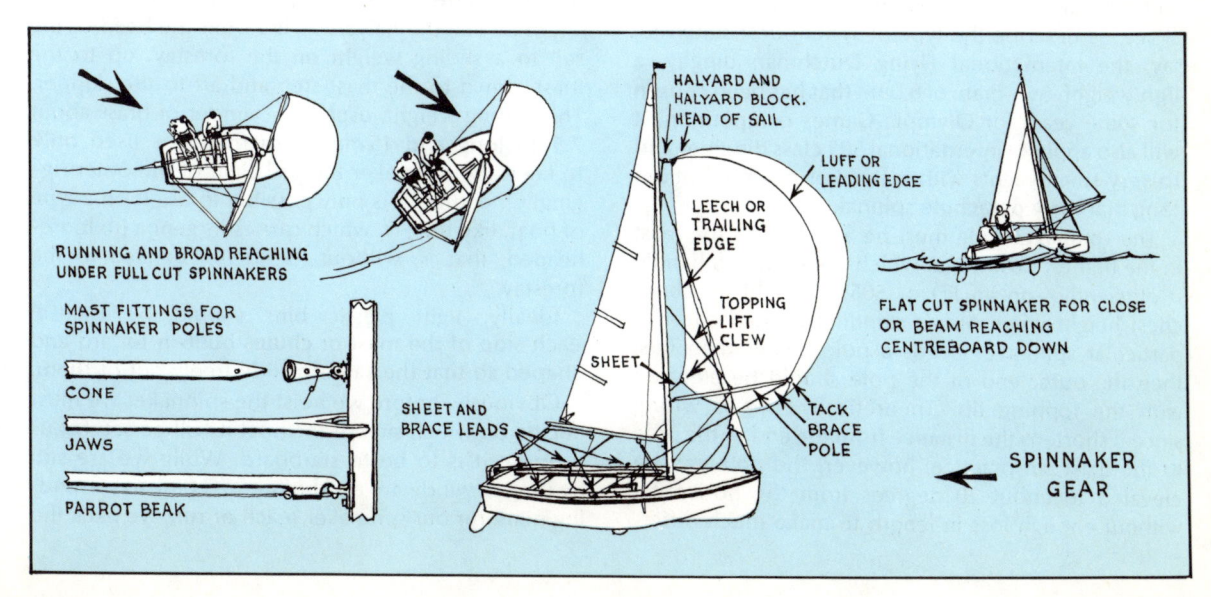

# LESSON 21
# Setting a spinnaker

Many beginners become flustered when they prepare to set a spinnaker because they try it in fresh breezes instead of practising in very light weather when the sail is easy to rig and control. There is a multiplicity of ways of rigging the brace and foreguy and of setting a spinnaker, but it is best to settle on one method to suit your boat. Then you should not vary it.

At first the best way to set a spinnaker is to hoist it 'in stops', that is with the luff and leech brought together, edge-to-edge, and the body of the sail rolled up to the edges and tied together like a string of sausages. Short lengths of light wool (two-ply is suitable) should be used for the stops, and tied no closer than 60 cm apart. They will break easily and fall clear when one pulls on the spinnaker sheet. This system allows the brace, foreguy, spinnaker pole, topping lift and sheet to be fastened up and all to be adjusted in their approximate 'set' positions without the sail filling with wind immediately it is hoisted. In very hard weather, particularly aboard ocean racers, even expert crews set their spinnakers in stops to prevent them tangling. For at least your first season of spinnaker handling you should set them in stops.

However, for speed, most racing crews in all types of boats set spinnakers 'flying', out of 'turtle bags', built-in 'bins' or plastic baskets attached to the foredeck or the leeward rigging. To these men, because of constant practice in hoisting and lowering spinnakers, it is as easy an exercise as tacking a boat.

In a racing boat you must have the best possible system of setting a spinnaker. The crewman or, if you sail a boat with more than one crewman, both or all of you, should be completely trained in this system. Then, whenever the wind angle makes it possible for a spinnaker to be carried to advantage, it can be set with no fear of being fouled up.

Let me describe the type of system best suited to, say, the international Flying Dutchman dinghy, a lightweight, two-man, of 6.09m that has been chosen for some years for Olympic Games competition. It will also apply to international 505 class dinghies and to very small yachts with spinnaker poles about 2m long that carry parachute spinnakers.

The spinnaker pole must be attached to the mast in the highest position at which the crew can handle it efficiently—on an FD or 505 it should be about chest height when one is standing in the boat. If a particular spinnaker needs a pole higher than this, then the outer end of the pole should be elevated with the topping lift. Theoretically, this is wrong since it shortens the distance from the end of the pole to the mast; in practice, however, the pole can be elevated to about 20 degrees from the horizontal without enough loss in length to make much difference. Having decided on the angle the pole should take, we must make it stay there with the topping lift and the foreguy.

On some racing dinghies the topping lift and foreguy are made up as one complete unit. A 1.5mm diameter wire, attached to the mast at the spreader fittings, comes down to the middle of the spinnaker pole, where it passes through a plastic fitting attached to the middle of the pole. This plastic fitting is shaped like a cleat with the horns turned back inwards instead of outwards. Two balls of metal are swaged (clamped by pressure) on to the wire about 15 cm apart on either side of the plastic fitting, thus limiting the rise and fall of the pole on the wire. The wire below the pole continues down to the mast just above the deck and passes through a small block. Spliced into the end of the wire is an eye through which is fastened a small shackle; the shoulders of this shackle act as a stop when the pole tries to lift. Also attached to the shackle is a piece of fabric-sheathed rubber (called shock cord) brought back up to the mast or along the deck and having just enough tension to pull the wire tight when the pole is taken down. The overall length of the wire should be enough to allow the inner end of the pole to be attached easily to the mast but not so long as to allow the pole to lift and get out of control.

The parrot beak fittings on the ends of the pole should be identical and there should be a short length of cord (without knots or loops that might catch on other parts of the rigging) on each of the beaks to allow them to be pulled open.

The spinnaker brace and spinnaker sheet, which must be identical, should be led aft through blocks on each corner of the transom and then forward to a place where the crew can control them.

On an FD, the halyard is led from the head of the sail to a sliding weight on the forestay, up to the mast, down to the mast-step and aft to the skipper. This sliding weight, usually a cylinder of brass about 7.5 cm long and 15 mm in diameter, is used only to keep the spinnaker halyard clear of the other rigging. Of course, it is only possible to use it on a type of boat, like the FD, which carries its genoa jib loose-headed, that is, without its jib luff hanked to the forestay.

Ideally, light plastic bins should be built-in each side of the mast or chutes built-in for'ard and shaped so that the sail can slide freely out of them.

Obviously, before we hoist the spinnaker we must decide on which side of the boat it will be set. Let us suppose it is to be to starboard. While we are still beating to windward and before we come to a rounding mark for our spinnaker reach or run, we pack the

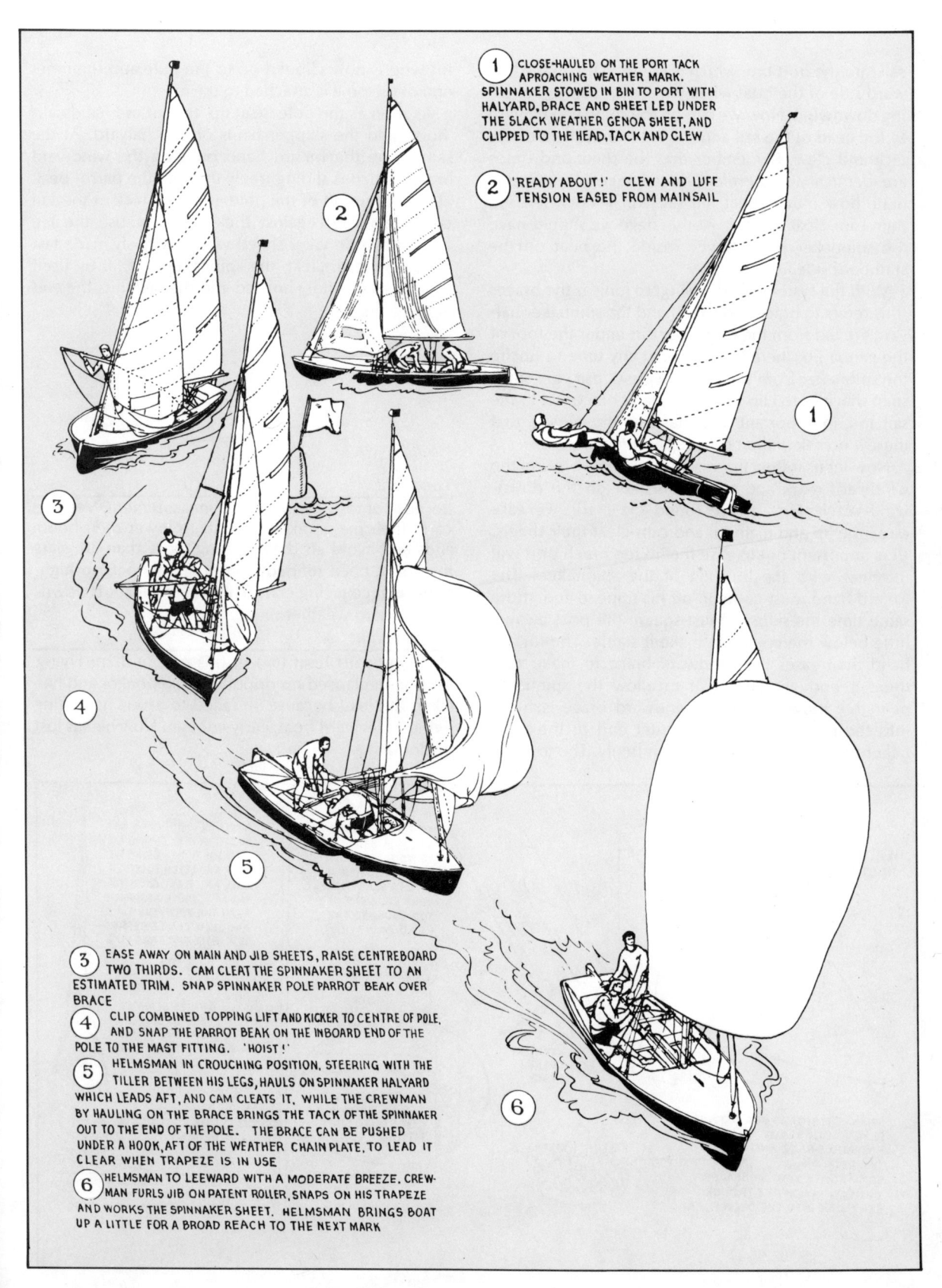

(1) CLOSE-HAULED ON THE PORT TACK APROACHING WEATHER MARK. SPINNAKER STOWED IN BIN TO PORT WITH HALYARD, BRACE AND SHEET LED UNDER THE SLACK WEATHER GENOA SHEET, AND CLIPPED TO THE HEAD, TACK AND CLEW

(2) 'READY ABOUT!' CLEW AND LUFF TENSION EASED FROM MAINSAIL

(3) EASE AWAY ON MAIN AND JIB SHEETS, RAISE CENTREBOARD TWO THIRDS. CAM CLEAT THE SPINNAKER SHEET TO AN ESTIMATED TRIM. SNAP SPINNAKER POLE PARROT BEAK OVER BRACE

(4) CLIP COMBINED TOPPING LIFT AND KICKER TO CENTRE OF POLE, AND SNAP THE PARROT BEAK ON THE INBOARD END OF THE POLE TO THE MAST FITTING. 'HOIST!'

(5) HELMSMAN IN CROUCHING POSITION, STEERING WITH THE TILLER BETWEEN HIS LEGS, HAULS ON SPINNAKER HALYARD WHICH LEADS AFT, AND CAM CLEATS IT. WHILE THE CREWMAN BY HAULING ON THE BRACE BRINGS THE TACK OF THE SPINNAKER OUT TO THE END OF THE POLE. THE BRACE CAN BE PUSHED UNDER A HOOK, AFT OF THE WEATHER CHAIN PLATE, TO LEAD IT CLEAR WHEN TRAPEZE IS IN USE

(6) HELMSMAN TO LEEWARD WITH A MODERATE BREEZE. CREWMAN FURLS JIB ON PATENT ROLLER, SNAPS ON HIS TRAPEZE AND WORKS THE SPINNAKER SHEET. HELMSMAN BRINGS BOAT UP A LITTLE FOR A BROAD REACH TO THE NEXT MARK

sail into the port bin, which is going to be on the leeward side of the boat when we are on course, reaching downwind. Now we clip on the spinnaker halyard to the head of the sail and the brace and sheet to the tack and clew. Remember that the sheet and brace are identical and therefore interchangeable. We estimate how much sheet the sail will need when set, then cam-cleat the rest. At this stage we should have the spinnaker pole stowed inside the boat on the starboard side.

With the system we are using, so long as the braces (this refers to brace *and* sheet) and the spinnaker halyard are led from the spinnaker out under the foot of the genoa jib, there is no need at any time to unclip the spinnaker from them. Some crews use very small snap shackles to clip the halyard and braces on to the sail and, in important races, tape up the clips so that there is no risk of their opening accidentally.

Now let us follow the various steps as we round the windward mark and set a spinnaker on the downwind reach. First, as we round the mark, we ease away the jib and mainsail and cam-cleat their sheets. (It is important not to ease the jib too much or it will interfere with the hoisting of the spinnaker.) The for'ard hand must come in off his trapeze and at the same time the skipper must square the boat away a little below the course to make it stable. The for'ard hand then eases the windward brace to make sure there is enough slack in it to allow the spinnaker pole free movement. The windward brace is fitted into the parrot beak on the outer end of the spinnaker pole; it must be able to run freely. The topping lift wire is now clipped on to the pole and the inner end of the pole is attached to the mast.

As soon as the pole is set up, the for'ard hand calls 'hoist' and the skipper hauls on the halyard. At the same time the for'ard hand pulls on the windward brace, which is sliding freely through the parrot beak at the outer end of the pole, until the tack of the sail comes up hard against the beak. Because the lee brace (the spinnaker sheet) was previously made fast in its own cam-cleat, the spinnaker will fill by itself as soon as it is fully hoisted and the tack hits the end of the pole.

*Top Right*
Because of restrictions on sail measurement, Vee Jays carry their masts raked well aft to lower their boom ends and avoid air drag. During more than 30 years they have been refined from training boats to high-performance racing craft. They touch 16 knots downwind in hard weather.

*Bottom Right*
The windward boat (64) of this pair of 3.2m Flying Ants has collapsed his opponent's spinnaker and has taken the lead because 90 failed to assert his luffing rights, as leeward boat, early enough. Now he has lost the initiative.

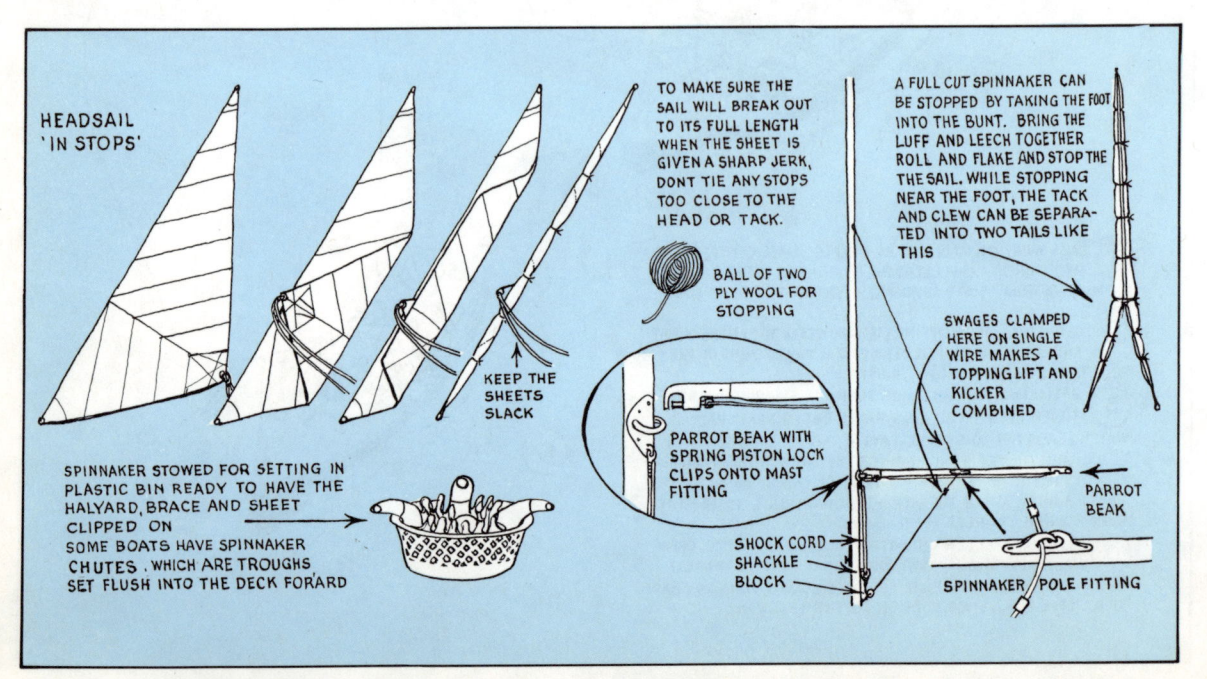

40

41

# LESSON 22
## Spinnaker trimming

With our FD spinnaker up and filled and its sheet made fast it will set 'shy' (suitable for a beam reach) without any immediate trimming. If the reach continues to be tight, as it should be when a proper Olympic-style course has been laid for the first downwind leg of the course, the for'ard hand should make the brace fast in its cam-cleat and then push the brace down under a hook fastened on the deck near the windward shroud. This hook keeps the brace down and also prevents it from fouling the trapeze. There is one problem with this hook system, however—it puts a lot of downward strain on the spinnaker pole, which therefore needs to have strength to spare.

The next job is to lift our centreboard to the right height to suit a reach and, if the weather is light, to adjust the vang under the mainsail boom to stop the boom lifting and distorting the mainsail shape. Had the wind been fresh from the start, the vang would have been set up earlier at about half-tension, and should not now need attention. If our spinnaker drill has gone entirely according to plan the whole operation will have taken only about twenty seconds.

With the boat on course the for'ard hand can roll up the genoa jib, usually with a patented furling device fastened on the tack—this can be operated by a line brought back into the cockpit—or, failing this, by hand. It is essential to furl the jib to prevent it from interfering with the set of the spinnaker. But it should never be necessary to lower the jib because while it is hoisted and unrolled it acts as a 'net' during the spinnaker setting and stops the spinnaker wrapping around itself and around the forestay. (On ocean racers, special spinnaker nets are sometimes rigged to prevent spinnakers fouling. Because of the size of many of these craft and the pressures that would be exerted on their rigging, patent jib-furling devices cannot be fitted to their forestays. Thus jibs often have to be lowered altogether to prevent them from interfering with the set of spinnakers.)

With the jib furled our FD for'ard hand should prepare to take the lee brace (the spinnaker sheet) from the helmsman, who will earlier have flicked this sheet out of its cam-cleat so that, if necessary, he could trim it to keep the sail drawing. With the spinnaker sheet in his hand, the for'ard hand is now free to get out on his trapeze. His job is to keep the sail presenting its best possible angle to the breeze. If the wind draws ahead a little he will have to harden in the sheet and probably ease the brace; if the wind comes astern he will have to haul on the brace and ease the sheet.

Below: On broad reaches these high performance 12-foot skiffs have spinnaker, jib, main set perfectly for the fresh breeze. The helmsman (foreground) is steering with a long extension rod from the tiller and holding the mainsheet in his teeth as he trapezes alongside his crewman. *Sydney Morning Herald*

Classical hiking technique for a 4.49m Finn dinghy. This sailor has his legs at just the right angle, knees over the centre of the side deck, body hooked with little strain on his stomach muscles, but is ready to extend himself outboard, as the breeze freshens, to balance the boat.

# LESSON 23
# Gybing and lowering a spinnaker

**Gybing the Spinnaker**

As our racing Flying Dutchman approaches the leeward mark it is time to prepare to gybe the spinnaker as the boat swings around on to the new course. If we are running fairly 'shy' on a beam reach it is advisable for the helmsman to edge up a little higher than the desired course, then square away for the mark.

The operation from then on is simple enough if a definite procedure is followed. All the for'ard hand has to do when he has swung inboard on his trapeze wire is:

1 Ease off the spinnaker sheet a metre or so and cam-cleat it again.
2 Unclip the spinnaker pole from the mast and pass the inner end of the pole *under* the slack leeward genoa jib sheet.
3 Clip what was the *inner* parrot beak (but is now going to be *outboard*) on to the spinnaker sheet which is going to become the brace.
4 Push out the pole.
5 Let the brace, which will become the sheet after the gybe, drop out of the parrot beak that was holding it and which is now inboard.
6 Clip the inner end of the pole to the mast.

Then, as the helmsman gybes the boat on to her new course and trims in the mainsheet, the for'ard hand can trim up his spinnaker brace and sheet.

**Lowering the Spinnaker**

When we have almost completed the spinnaker reach it is important to get the sail down swiftly so that we can come on a wind without losing time or distance.

If we are still running fairly 'shy', the helmsman should again edge up to windward as he approaches the rounding mark so that he can square away (as he did for gybing) for the operation of lowering the spinnaker. The genoa jib should then be unrolled to help prevent the spinnaker from fouling the forestay or wrapping around itself. (It does not matter if the genoa jib is not setting properly at this stage.) Now we must lower the centreboard ready for the ensuing beat to windward.

The spinnaker brace should be flicked free from its cam-cleat, so that both it and the spinnaker sheet can be held by the for'ard hand in *one* hand, while he judges the distance from the mark. Next, with his free hand, the for'ard hand unclips the inner end of the spinnaker pole from the mast and holds the pole firmly. He should also slip the windward sheet of the genoa jib over his head and keep it draped across the back of his neck, where it will be clear of the spinnaker. Meanwhile, the helmsman should make sure that the spinnaker halyard is clear of tangles and spread loosely on the floor of the boat, ready to let go.

When it is time to lower the spinnaker, the for'ard hand lets go both the brace and the sheet, pulls in the spinnaker pole, unclips it from the topping lift and passes it back for the helmsman to stow. As he passes the pole aft he must take hold of the spinnaker brace and unclip it from the parrot beak on the end of the pole. Immediately, the helmsman lets the spinnaker halyard run free. Then the fastest way for the for'ard hand to stow the spinnaker is to stand up and pull it all down to windward so that it becomes a bundle he can stuff into the windward bin in one positive movement. He now needs only to bow his head forward so that the genoa jib sheet falls off his neck, before he hooks on his trapeze again and hikes out to windward as far as required, trimming the genoa sheet as he goes. The whole operation may seem a job for more than two men but it can easily be done with constant practice at timing and co-operation.

There are, of course, numerous other layouts of spinnaker gear and methods of setting and lowering them on dinghies and yachts of different kinds. On yachts it is best to bring the spinnaker down to leeward by first easing the brace and later lowering the pole.

The beginner in sailing, for whom these lessons are intended, should, on joining a seasoned racing crew, carefully study the system used aboard and adapt himself to it. When the crew is not under the pressure of a race he should ask the for'ard hand to explain and demonstrate to him any points of the layout or technique that he does not understand. If he is starting off as the only for'ard hand in a small boat with a similarly inexperienced helmsman, and if, after constant practice in light weather, he cannot devise an efficient technique for handling the spinnaker, he should seek the advice of the best for'ard hand in his club in the same class of boat. It may be just a slight lack of manual dexterity that he needs to overcome. There is warm camaraderie among yachtsmen and it is a rare occasion when one will not go out of his way to help an enthusiastic beginner.

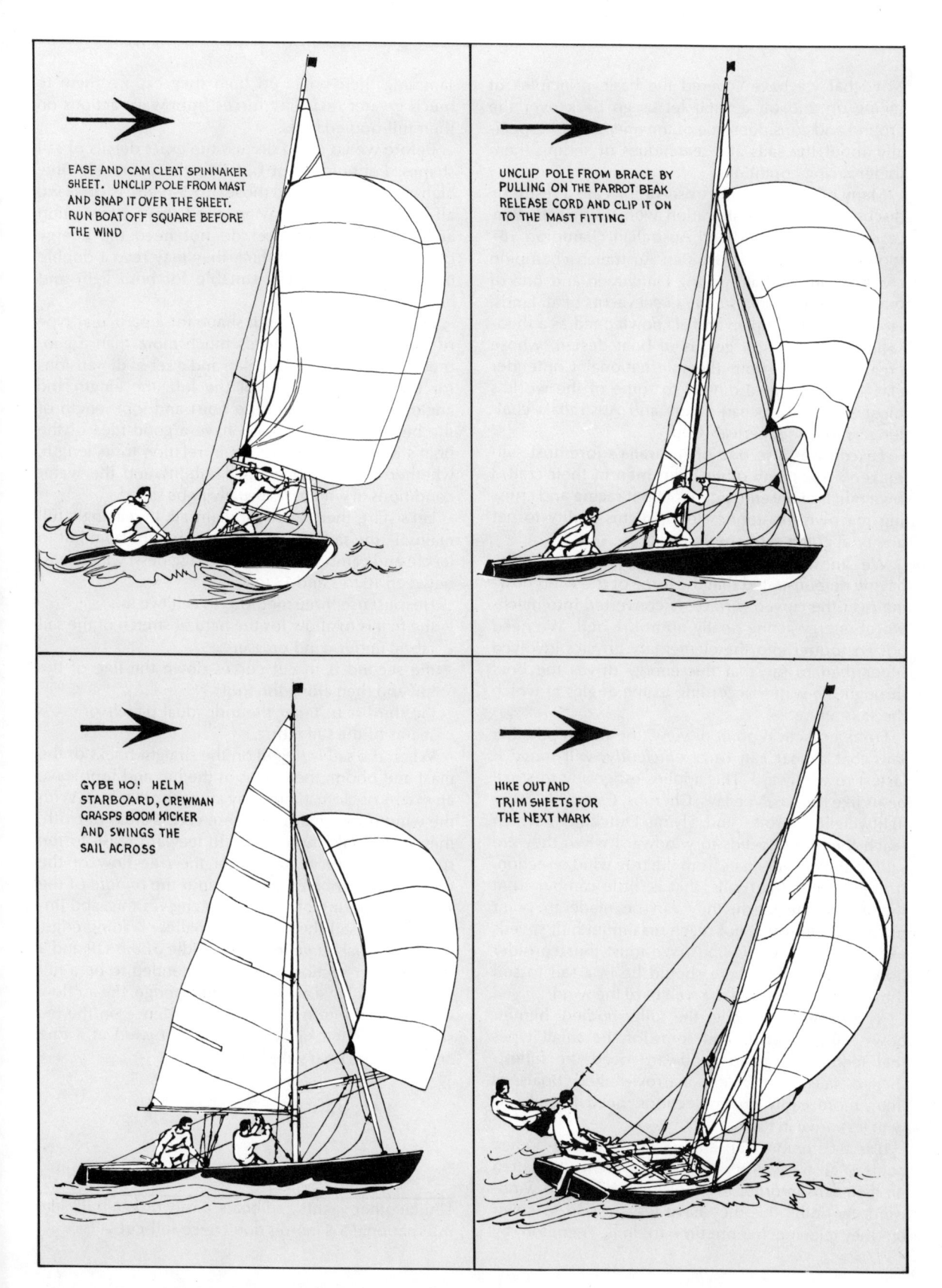

→ EASE AND CAM CLEAT SPINNAKER SHEET. UNCLIP POLE FROM MAST AND SNAP IT OVER THE SHEET. RUN BOAT OFF SQUARE BEFORE THE WIND

→ UNCLIP POLE FROM BRACE BY PULLING ON THE PARROT BEAK RELEASE CORD AND CLIP IT ON TO THE MAST FITTING

→ GYBE HO! HELM STARBOARD, CREWMAN GRASPS BOOM KICKER AND SWINGS THE SAIL ACROSS

→ HIKE OUT AND TRIM SHEETS FOR THE NEXT MARK

# LESSON 24
## Sails and sail handling

Now that we have covered the basic principles of sailing on and off a wind let us go back over the ground and consider some of the finer points, especially about the sails and techniques of setting them under racing conditions.

Many of the following observations are a result of discussions and collaboration with my friend, Ben Lexcen, former world and Australian champion 18-footer helmsman, for years an Australian champion crewman in Stars and Flying Dutchmen and one of our outstanding helmsmen in keel yachts of all kinds. He is a dual Olympian and acknowledged as a theoretical and practical genius of boat design, whose creations range from the international Contender class single-handed dinghy to some of the world's most successful ocean racers and Australia's challengers for the America's Cup.

Lexcen was also one of Australia's foremost sailmakers; like many other helmsmen in their craft, I owe much of my enjoyment of boat racing and cruising my own 4½-tonne sloop, to his ability to get any boat going at her best.

We know that the boat's sails are its engine, having demonstrated that the force of the wind flowing over the curved surfaces is converted into mechanical energy acting finally upon the hull. We need not go further into the elementary physics involved other than to say that this energy drives the boat through the water, according to the angles at which the sails are set.

From a practical point of view, the fullest possible sails that a boat can carry *efficiently*, will move it fastest to windward. This applies especially to small boats like Herons, Vee Jays, Cherubs, Gwen 12s, 505s, lightweight Sharpies and Flying Dutchmen, which reach their best speeds to windward when they are sailing about 45 degrees from the true wind direction. If they have flat-cut sails, that is, little camber from the luff to the leech, they can be made to point higher, but they will not reach maximum hull speeds except in very heavy winds. We must thus consider how much camber there should be in a sail to suit the shape of a boat and the weight of the wind.

As a general principle, the fuller-bodied, blunter bow-sectioned boats and some of the small types that tend to plane to windward need the fullest-shaped sails. Conversely, narrow-hulled boats of finer, more easily driven sections, need flatter sails with less drive in them.

It is a common fault among crews of full-bodied boats of all types, from dinghies to yachts, to flatten on their sails in order to point them higher to windward. By doing this they have less ground to cover but they take much more time to do it. Then, too, by jamming their boats up high they expose them to much greater retarding forces from wave actions on their full-bodied hulls.

Before we go on to discuss the exact details of sail shapes, I should point out that the extremely fine, high-pointing hulls like those of 5.5-metre yachts (and all the metre boats having good wave penetration and low hull resistance) do not need the energy created by full sails. In fact, they may reap a double benefit from a flat sail suitable for both light and heavy wind conditions.

So, in considering a sail shape for a particular type of boat, a sailmaker needs much more than a geometric outline of the sail plan and a set of dimensions for the rig—the height of the luff, the length and angle of the boom and the hoist and foot length of the headsail. He must also have a good idea of the boat's hull shape, its weight in relation to its length, whether it has high or low stability and the water conditions in which it is usually to be sailed.

Let's start, then, with the mainsail. In making a full mainsail, the sailmaker plans for a width (from luff to leech) and camber (or depth of bagginess) with a ratio between 10 to 1 and 13 to 1.

He must use three methods to achieve this:
the first is to allow for the natural stretch of the sail fabric under wind pressure;
the second is to cut curves down the line of the luff and then along the foot;
the third is to taper the individual panels or cross seams of the sail fabric.

When the sail is rigged on the straight tracks of the mast and boom, the curves in the luff and foot leave an excess of cloth all the way along those edges. With the wind pressing against these excess areas of cloth, they would take up a curve to leeward close to the spars—such curves can upset the free flow of the wind and must be coaxed out into the *middle* of the sail. The tapering of the seams achieves this, and imparts to the sail the necessary shallow leading edge, with a gradual curve into the middle of the sail and a straight after-section. If what is intended to be a full sail does not have a shallow *leading* edge, the air flow will break down in an area of turbulence on the lee side, so that the sail will not accept wind at a fine angle and the boat will slow up.

---

Unlike other yachts and boats, easily driven hulls like international 5.5 metres don't need full-cut sails.

46

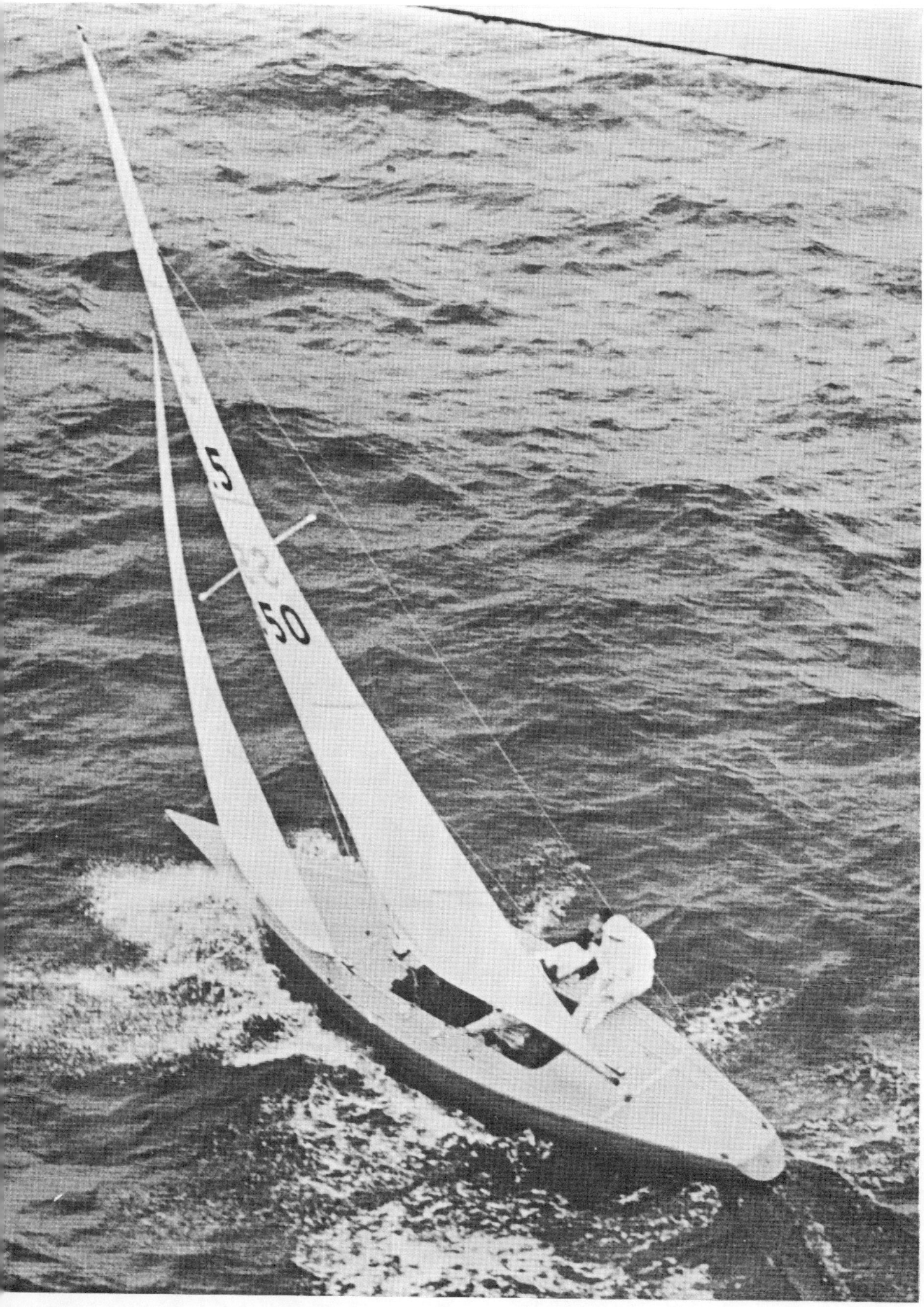

# LESSON 25
# Setting up the mainsail

Let us now consider, step by step, the correct methods one should use to set up a mainsail on a boat and get it working properly.

First, the mainsail should be rigged on to the boom and, when the tack is attached at the gooseneck, hauled out firmly along the foot until the wrinkles running vertically from the luff just disappear. Take care, however, not to drag the foot out to the point where the material begins to buckle horizontally along the boom or you will distort the sail and cause unequal tensions all over it.

When the battens are fitted snugly into the pockets and the luff slides are on the track (or, if you have an internal track, when the luff rope is led in), hoist the sail. Get a firm tension on the luff, but again be careful that it is not so tight that you set up a series of vertical corrugations in the material.

Does the sail have a crease spreading out from the tack into the body of the sail? If so, the gooseneck fitting might be pulling the corner of the sail down too far, or it is possible that the eye of the tack may be too far away from the mast. By alternately easing the main halyard and moving the tack back and forward, then re-hoisting, you will find the spot where the tack area of the sail takes up the best unwrinkled shape. To achieve this permanently, it may be necessary to move the point of fastening on the gooseneck fitting or to put in a shackle to extend the scope of the fastening. (Small boat sailors should not have to worry much about this, because there are a number of gooseneck fittings on the market with adequate adjustments.)

When the tack area is set up nicely, look at the clew of the sail. Generally, the clew eye (or cringle) should be on the same plane as the rest of the foot of the sail: it is essential that it is not too high or too low. If your boat is a yacht with a sail slide track on the foot, you should use an extra strong slide lashed to the clew cringle and make sure that this also allows the clew of the sail to lie on the same plane as the rest of the foot.

Now look at the headboard of the sail. Is it in line with the rest of the sail? If the halyard is pulling the headboard away from the mast there will be a distinct wrinkle (or a series of them) from the bottom of the headboard to the top batten. This should not happen if you have an internal track in the mast, but it often does with other types of tracks, especially when halyard sheaves are not properly set in the masthead. This causes the halyard, when under tension, to pull at an angle which prevents the eye in the headboard from remaining at the same distance from the mast as the eyelets in the sail to which the slides are attached. If your halyard is right and there are no wrinkles from the headboard, the next thing to check is the leech of the sail.

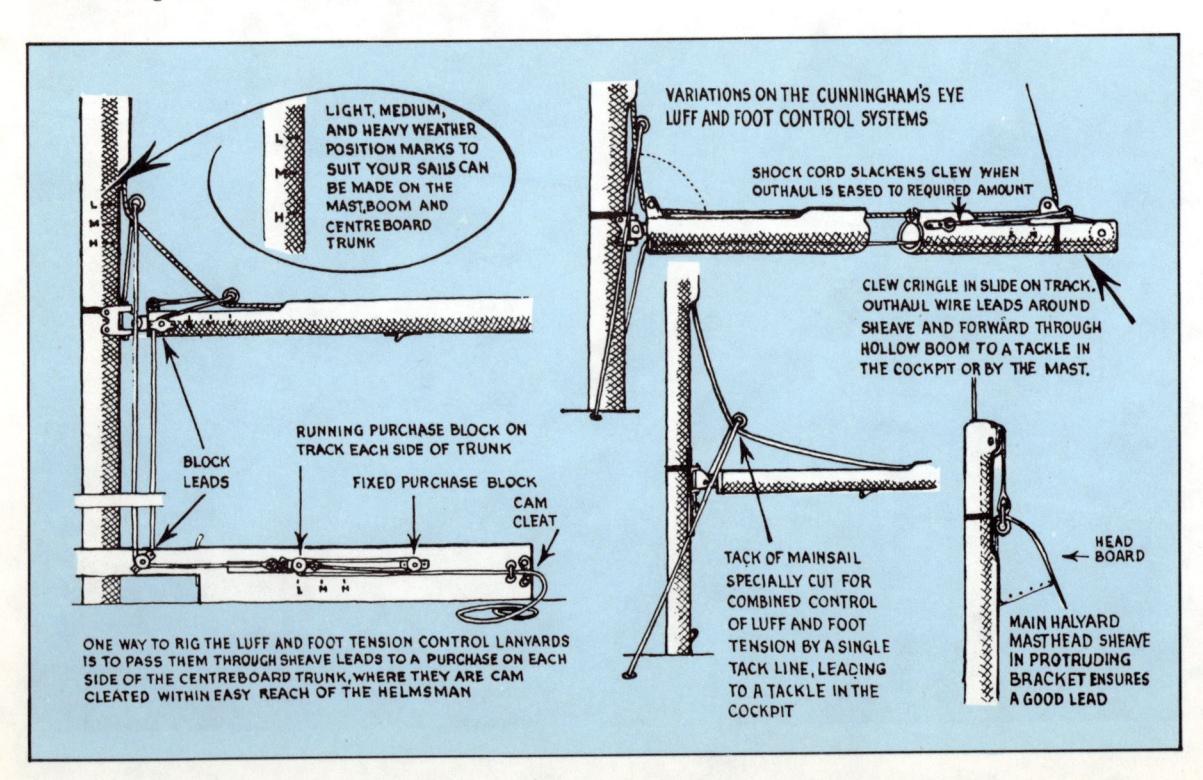

Knowledge and strict observance of steering rules adds excitement to close-quarters sailing. The youngsters in the Manly Juniors (above) are in a clearly defined windward-leeward situation. The windward boat must keep clear. The 12-foot skiff (below) approaches the rounding buoy on right-of-way starboard tack and yachts on port tack must keep clear provided the skiff holds course. *WA Newspapers and Sydney Morning Herald*

# LESSON 26
# Leech adjustments

The essential thing to know about the leech is that it should set without curling and so allow an uninterrupted flow of air from the windward and leeward sides of the sail.

Battens are generally used to help set the leech—let us consider them first. To test whether they are fitting correctly, pull on the main sheet until the sail is in the 'on a wind' position. If the battens tend to push a bump into the sail at their inner ends they may be too long. Make sure that they just fit into the pockets with about 8 mm of slack.

Most small boat and small yacht sails having four short battens should have the top two made so that they are reasonably thin and flexible at the inner ends and fairly stiff at the outer (leech) ends. The two lower battens should generally be only slightly tapered at the inner ends and stiff all the way.

If your boat is a yacht like a Dragon, of a type that allows the spinnaker sheet to jump over the end of the boom and press into the leech of the mainsail, the bottom batten should be very strong and should be sewn into the pocket so that it can't spring out.

Should you still find bumps in the sail after thinning down the battens and checking them for length it is possible that the sail has too much roach in it or that the leech is too tight. It may be possible to adjust this merely by easing the leech line, if you have one in the sail, but it could be a job for the sailmaker.

If the sail has full-length battens they should be shaped so that they *all* put an even tension on the sail and there is no sudden change in the curved shape of the sail. The best way to test this in a small boat is to lay it, with the mainsail rigged, on its side and adjust the battens one by one, until you have the sail curving evenly.

Now we are ready to put the sail to its real test—in the wind.

*Top Right*
The heavier crewman in the windward 3.2m Flying Ant is crouched only just outboard to keep his boat on her feet but the smaller boy in the leeward dinghy needs to use his trapeze as 221 rides through on a gust. *WA Newspapers*

*Bottom Right*
Use of trapeze harnesses rigged to wires from the mast has revolutionised 12-foot skiff sailing, making it possible for two-man crews to handle these most difficult of boats that once needed twice the weight in live ballast on the gunwale. *Sydney Morning Herald*

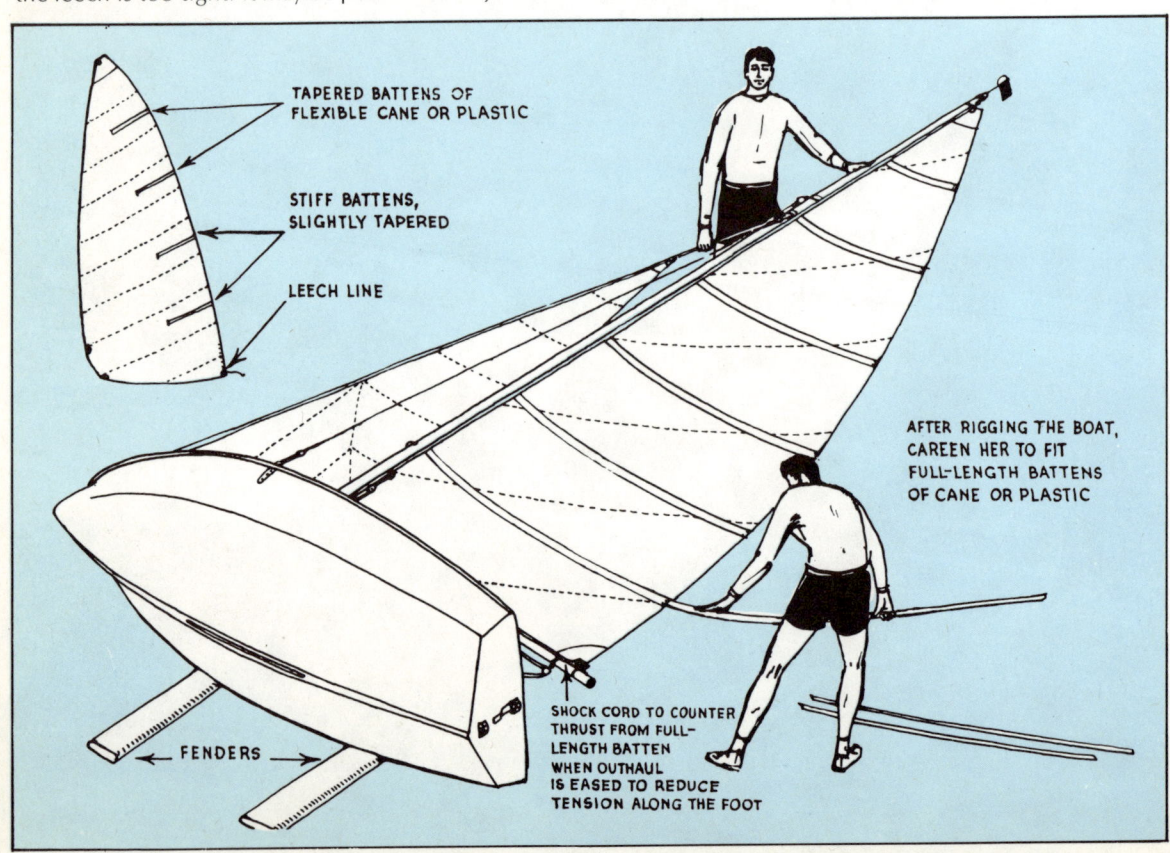

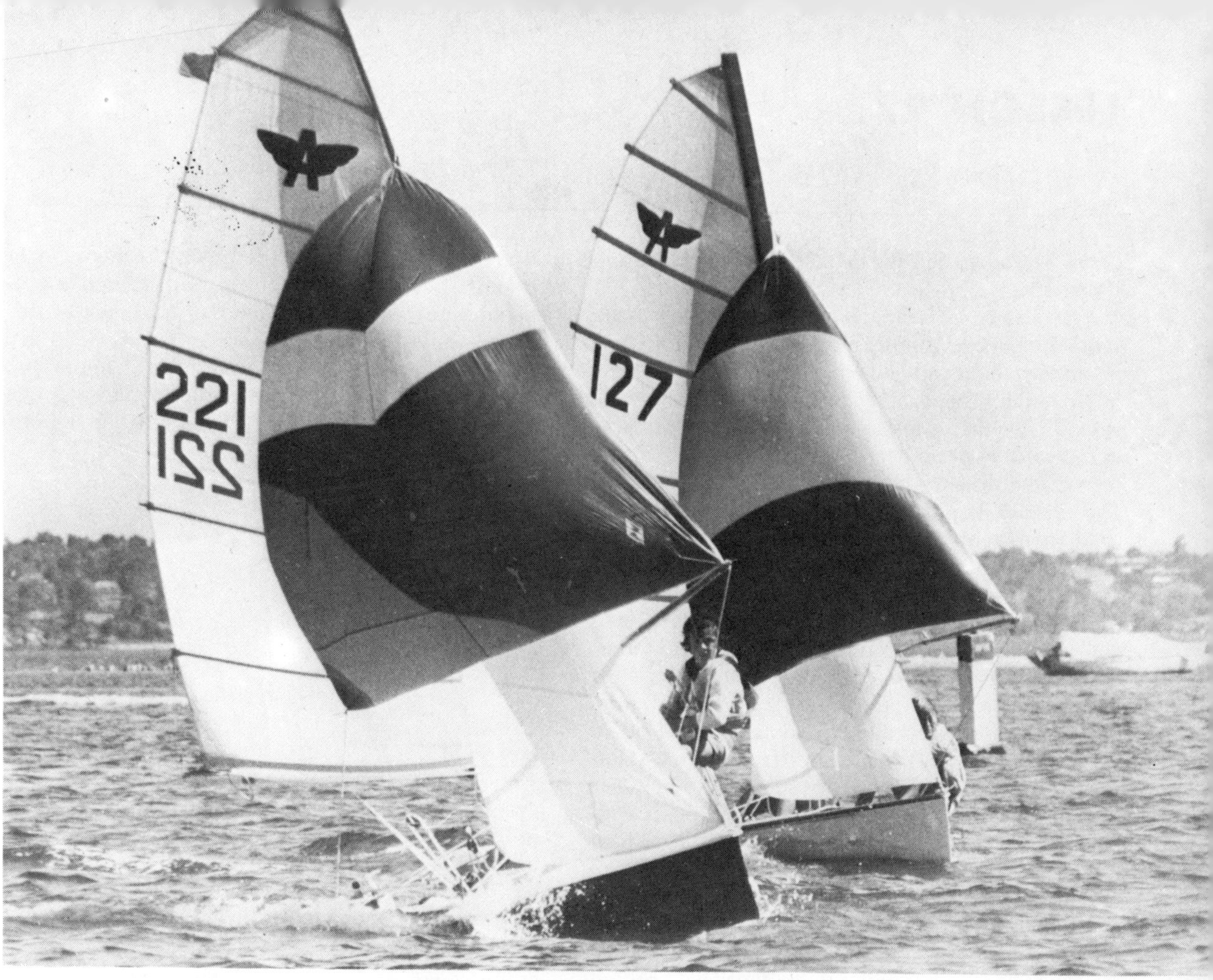
221
127

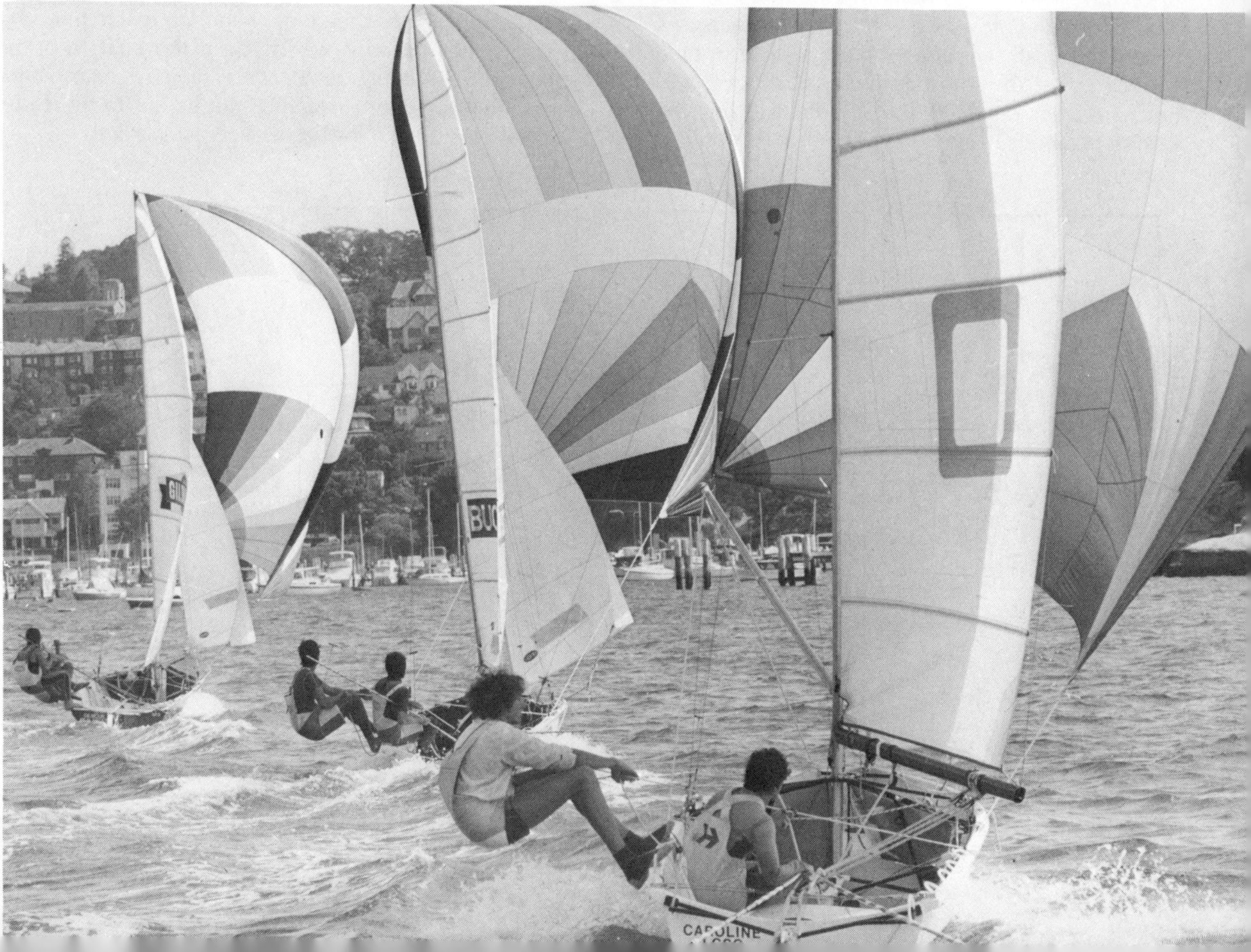
CAROLINE

# LESSON 27
## Camber of mainsails

Let us begin by checking that the mainsail really suits the boat.

If you carry an overlapping genoa jib, the mainsail should have different characteristics from that made for a boat carrying an ordinary jib which does not overlap. The mainsail with an overlapping jib should have the deepest part of its camber (or curve to leeward) high up near the head and 40 to 50 per cent of the distance back from the luff to the leech. This camber should not extend downwards in a vertical line towards the boom but sweep down to a shallower camber half-way back, along the fore and aft line, in the lower portion of the sail.

The boat with an ordinary jib and cat-rigged boats without jibs (such as Contenders, Moths and Finns) should also have the deepest part of the camber of the mainsail 40 to 50 per cent of the way back from the luff to the leech. But this should extend down vertically all the way from the head to the foot. Mainsails for boats with ordinary jibs should also be fuller coming off the boom than mainsails for boats with overlapping genoa jibs. Adjustments to mainsails of boats with ordinary jibs and cat-rigged boats are much more critical than to those with genoa jibs, although the same principles can be observed.

If your boat is a modern racing yacht its mainsail should have a zipper built into the foot enabling you to flatten the sail as the wind strength increases. If it is of the small centreboard class, instead of there being a zipper, the boom should be flexible: it will need to be bent down in the middle by the sheeting system, about 10 cm for every 3 m of length, in order to flatten the mainsail as the breeze freshens. Yacht booms should ideally be fitted with adequate outhauling gear so that the mainsail foot may be adjusted while the boat is sailing on the wind. So that the luff can be tightened or eased, the boom also needs an adequate gooseneck adjustment system, or a 'Cunningham Eye' tackle, or a combination of both.

*Top Right*
The 4m OK dinghy in the foreground is squared away with his sheet well eased and his boat, planing in the squall, is under control. Note the bend of his unstayed mast. But in the background the man in 282 has failed to ease his sheet and pull away and his boat's chine, digging in, is driving him off course up to windward.

*Bottom Right*
Planing at high speed on a broad reach this OK dinghy helmsman is well back in the boat to bring the centre of lateral resistance as far aft as he can and maintain directional stability. But he has to be ready to ease his sheet if the breeze gets any harder.

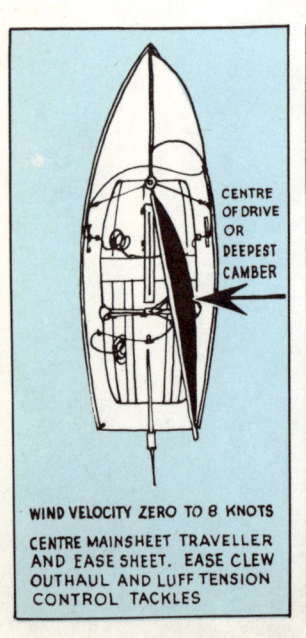

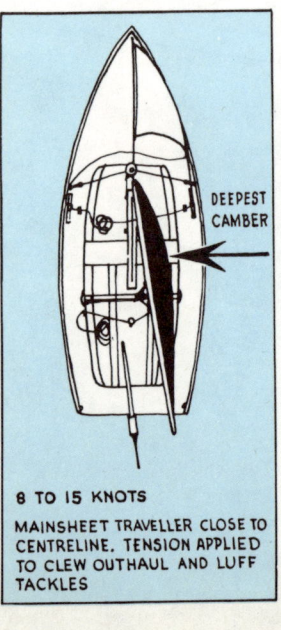

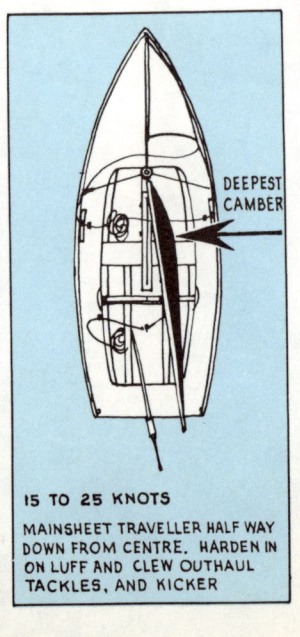

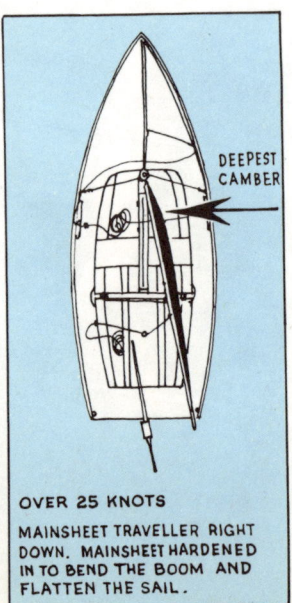

**WIND VELOCITY ZERO TO 8 KNOTS**
CENTRE MAINSHEET TRAVELLER AND EASE SHEET. EASE CLEW OUTHAUL AND LUFF TENSION CONTROL TACKLES

**8 TO 15 KNOTS**
MAINSHEET TRAVELLER CLOSE TO CENTRELINE. TENSION APPLIED TO CLEW OUTHAUL AND LUFF TACKLES

**15 TO 25 KNOTS**
MAINSHEET TRAVELLER HALF WAY DOWN FROM CENTRE. HARDEN IN ON LUFF AND CLEW OUTHAUL TACKLES, AND KICKER

**OVER 25 KNOTS**
MAINSHEET TRAVELLER RIGHT DOWN. MAINSHEET HARDENED IN TO BEND THE BOOM AND FLATTEN THE SAIL.

53

# LESSON 28
## Adjusting the mainsail – light conditions

In winds up to eight knots the zipper in the foot of a yacht's sail should be undone to make the mainsail very full along the foot. In a small boat, the mainsheeting system should be arranged so that the boom is not bending in the middle and flattening the sail. The luff of the sail should also be adjusted so that the deepest part of the camber is half-way back in the sail from the luff to the leech. The foot adjustments at the clew should be eased until there is quite a bag of loose cloth along the boom, and the outer end of the bottom batten of the sail pokes up to windward of the boom.

With the basic adjustments made, the next most important step is to trim the mainsheet on its traveller. This should be close to the centre of the boat and the mainsheet should be eased off as much as possible without losing wind pressure in the sail or having to point too far 'off' the wind. Special care must be taken to ensure that the boat is not 'oversheeted' when the mainsail is adjusted with such fullness, otherwise this will kill the boat's speed through the water.

We must also consider the water conditions in which we are sailing. If the boat is in *very* smooth water, the sail should not be set to the maximum fullness that our adjustments allow. However, the sail should be set with a lot of fullness, as we have earlier described, in rough or lumpy water conditions, such as we get offshore or in harbours with waves set up by lots of boats moving in a congested area.

The best way to find the absolutely correct trim in these light conditions is to race alongside a boat with a similar performance to your own and adjust each section of your mainsail—the luff, the foot, the mainsheet traveller, the zipper (or boom bend) and the sheeting tension. As you make each of these adjustments, carefully check your boat's performance relative to that of your opponent until you find those which establish a definite improvement in speed. Remember that each small adjustment must be made *separately* to avoid confusion. Sometimes you might have to sail for a kilometre or more on the one tack to evaluate properly the change you have made. This is a long, tedious business that may take weeks of testing, especially if your boat is sailing at near its full potential when you start: but, ultimately, it is worth it, if you want to get your boat in a high state of tune.

When you have decided on the best adjustments to your mainsail for light weather conditions, record them by marking the mainsheet with coloured threads and the spars and other points of adjustment with paint or marking ink, so that you can readily put the gear back into the same trim.

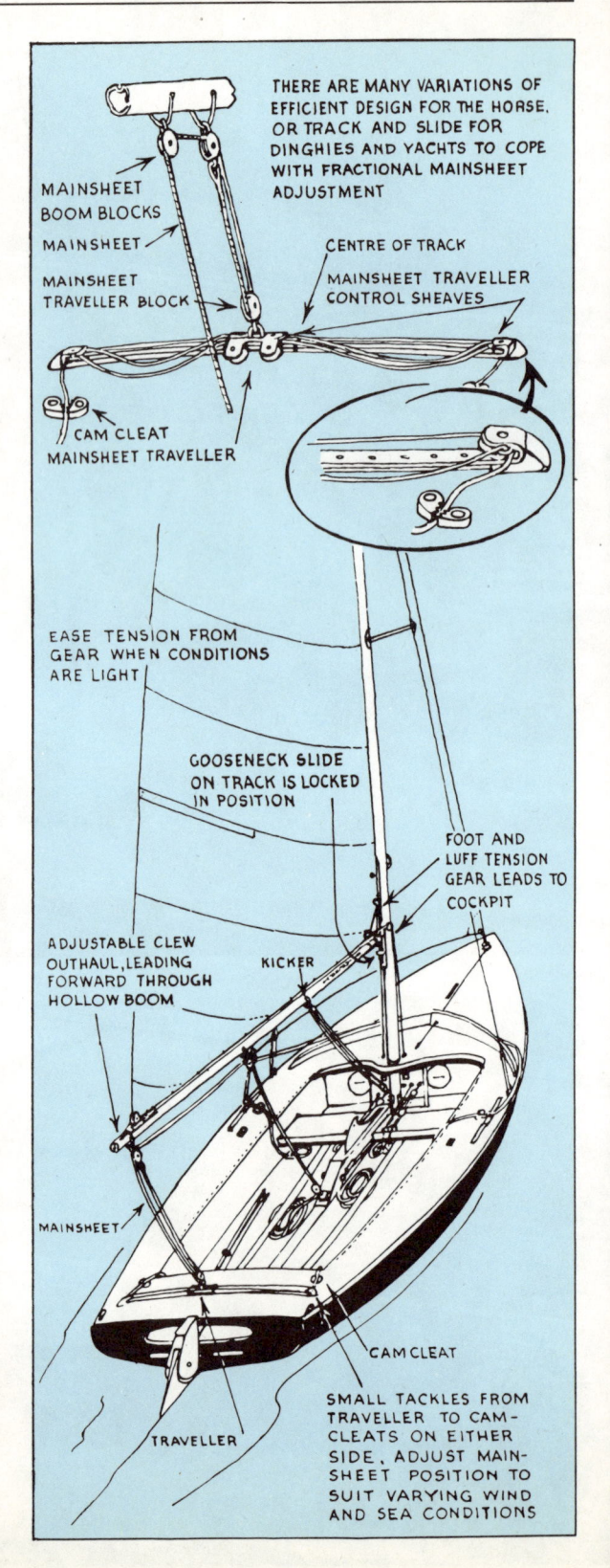

A sound knowledge of the racing rules and a capacity for instant decisions is essential when racing in close company. Two of these 3.66m Cherub class dinghies (607 and 1073) are already round the turning mark and on starboard tacks demanding their right of way over the port tackers.

Moths: In a mass start the 'safe' leeward end of the line is often the best place to be, provided you can get clear air and are not blanketed by boats to windward. But a slight misjudgment of distance in the final few seconds before the gun can be disastrous.

# LESSON 29
# Adjusting the mainsail — fresh conditions

As the wind increases from 8 to 15 knots the mainsail should be pulled down on the luff and tightened along the foot so that the camber moves for'ard of the central area. Sheet in the sail a little harder, too, but only enough to compensate for the stretch in the sail and the sheet rope. The curve of the leech of the sail should be maintained in the same position as in light weather. In a yacht the best way to judge this curve is to estimate how far from the permanent backstay the leech of the sail would be if it were extended aft. In some small boats without permanent backstays you must depend on observations—the distance of the end of the boom from the gunwale can be a useful guide.

As the breeze increases from 15 to 25 knots, the mainsail should be pulled out to its maximum on the foot and down on the luff enough to bring the camber forward to about one-third of the fore and aft distance from the luff to the leech. The mainsheet traveller-stops should be eased out and, if you have an adjustable backstay, it should be tightened to bend the mast a little and so flatten the mainsail. In small boats, whatever system is used to bend the mast should also be employed to flatten the mainsail.

Over 25 knots the mainsheet traveller should be eased out to the limit, to the full width of the boat if possible. The mainsail should also be sheeted down hard, the zipper closed (or the boom bent down in the middle) to flatten the mainsail, and the backstay, if adjustable, pulled on hard.

In squalls the boat should be sailed high into the wind to prevent her heeling excessively.

But one word of warning. If your boat has a genoa jib don't ease the mainsail traveller out so far as in a boat with a small jib, or you will 'choke' the headsail, that is, prevent the free escape of the wind from it, and your boat will slow up and stagger.

### Right

Few yachtsmen ever achieve all-round excellence in so many fields of sailing as Australia's late Ben Lexcen, here demonstrating trapeze technique on a 4.87-metre Contender. This single-handed class is one of a string of craft, ranging to giant ocean racers, of Lexcen's design. He was also an expert sailmaker, inventor of yachting equipment, outstanding crewman, helmsman of rare ability, and created America's Cup winner *Australia* II.

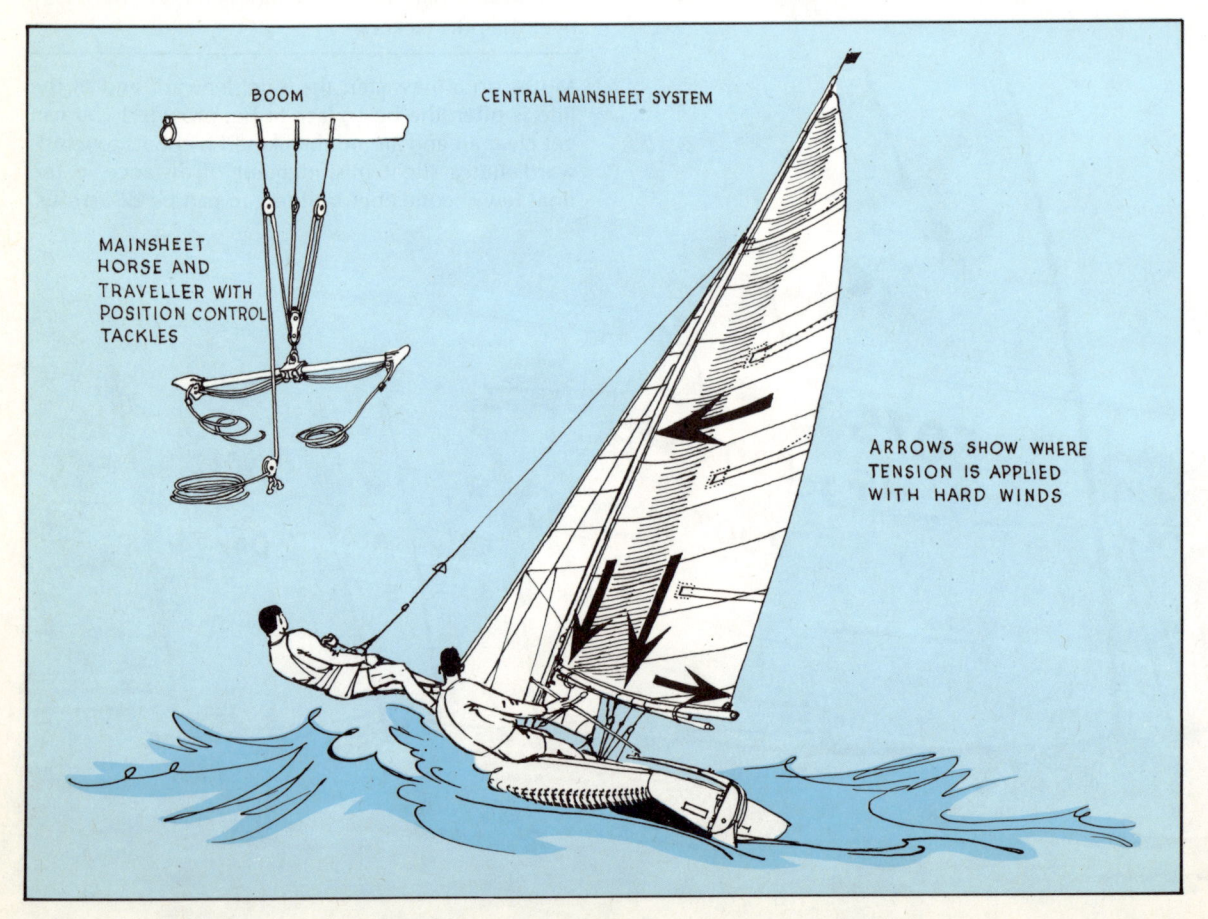

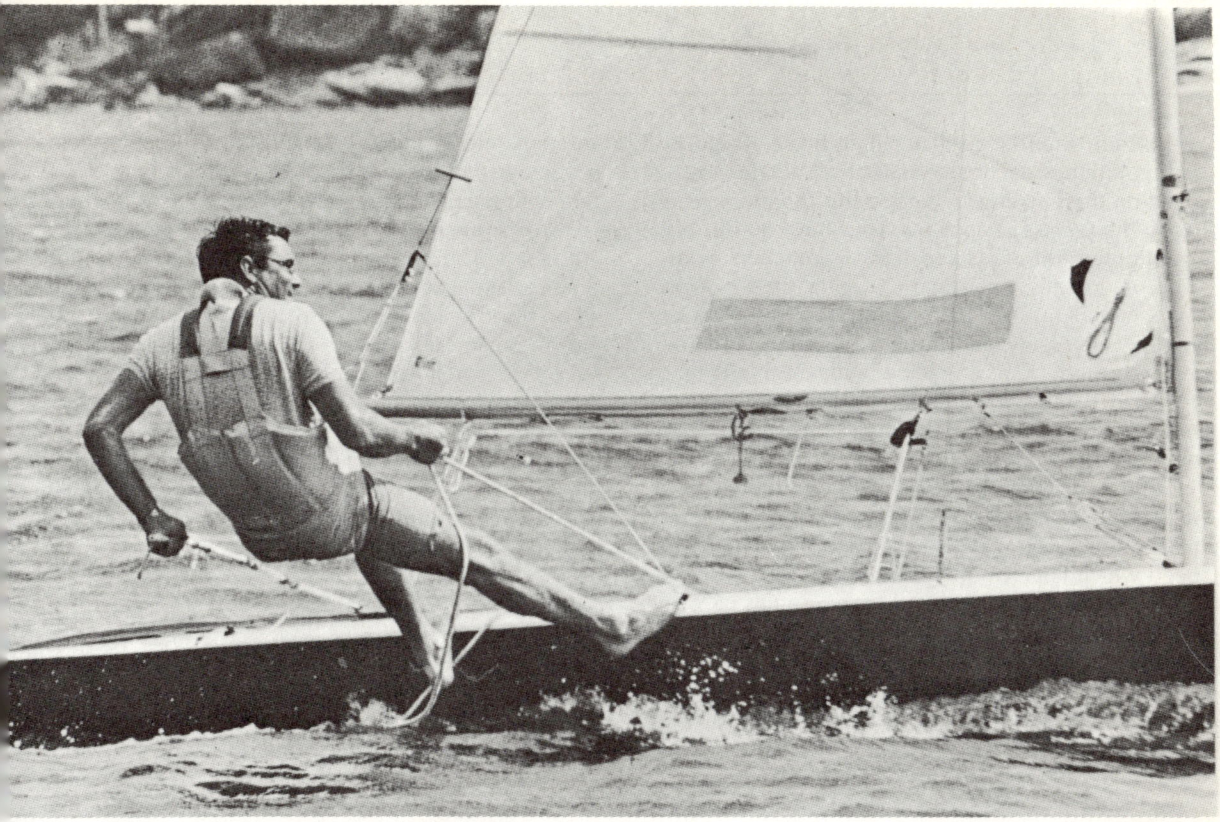

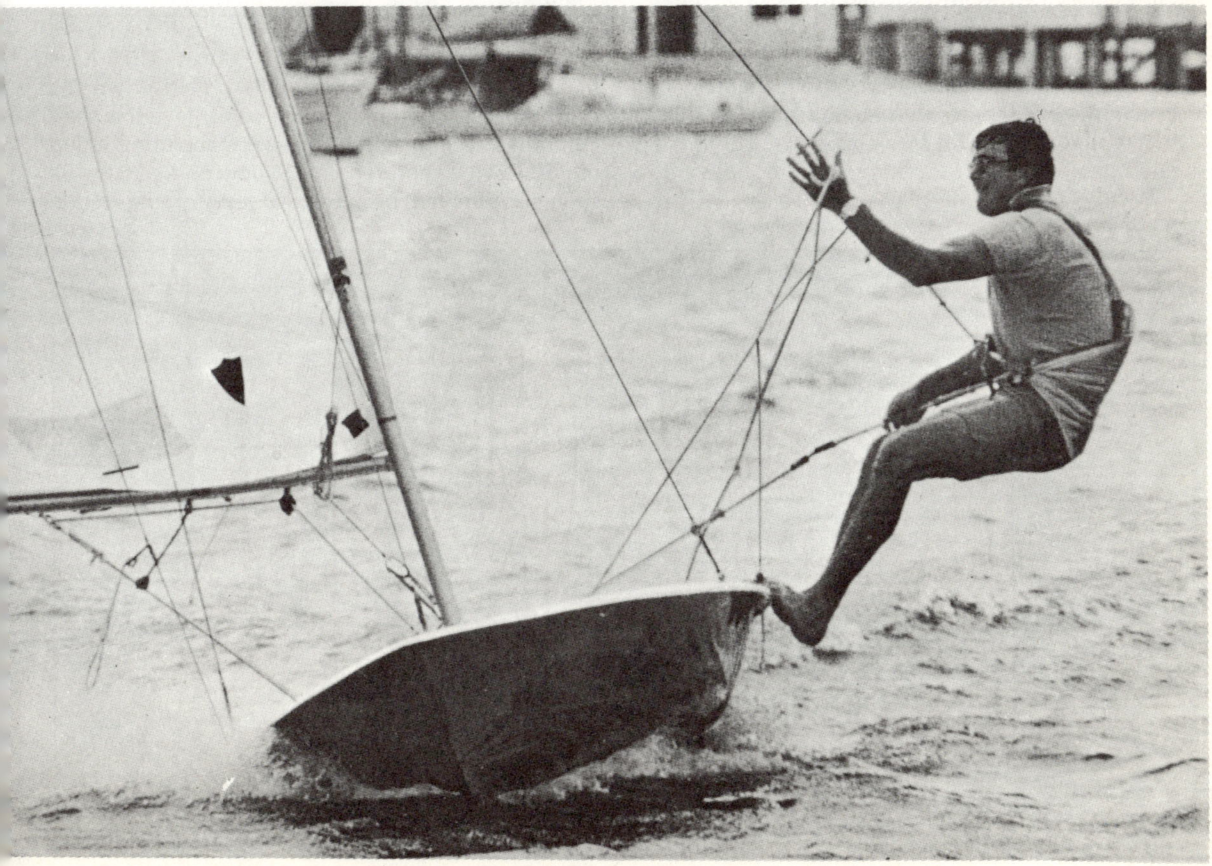

# LESSON 30
# Headsails and their uses

Yachtsmen often argue that sailing boats would be better off if they did not have jibs at all but depended solely on their mainsails. We see this theory in practice in the C class catamarans. They have no jibs but gigantic aerofoil masts and narrow, roached mainsails; or no sails, only rigid, tapering flaps behind wing-shaped masts. Undoubtedly for this class of hull they are highly efficient. On the other hand, the trend for modern ocean racing boats, until changes in the rules imposed some inhibitions, was to have enormous jibs overlapping their masts and very small mainsails.

Neither of these cases settles the argument very well. Both rigs have evolved from special circumstances. The C class catamarans reach a very high top speed which largely nullifies use of a jib. The ocean racing measurement and handicapping rules gave as a free bonus, and still give to some extent, much of the sail area set from the fore side of the mast, and thus designers take advantage of it.

Perhaps I should explain that in the case of the catamarans the speed of the boat creates an apparent wind which is almost dead in line with its course. Thus it is almost impossible to sheet on a jib sufficiently to preserve an aerofoil shape and so allow the sail to exhaust the wind from it. But this is an extreme case.

Most boats, from dinghies up, need jibs of some kind, so let us consider the best way to use them.

One of the good things about a jib is that, area for area, it is more efficient than a mainsail when both are sheeted in and the boat is sailing close to the wind. Despite the fact that a jib does not have as good an aerodynamic profile as a mainsail, it has the great advantage that there is no mast in front of it to interfere with the clean flow of wind on to and off its surfaces. However, this situation changes when sheets are eased. The jib, having no vang to hold its foot down as a mainsail does, twists into an inferior shape when close reaching. It also tends to exhaust wind into the mainsail and to reduce its efficiency. But at least it does help to balance the steering of the boat, especially one which has no moveable lateral plane, such as a centreboard. By trimming the jib in a little harder when close reaching and easing the mainsail, the weather helm can be largely reduced. We must learn to live with our jibs and take the good with the bad.

*Right*
No single-hulled craft can pace it with the twin-hulled catamarans on a reach and they attain such high speed that often they draw the apparent wind 60 degrees ahead of its true direction. To mono-hull sailors, the big cats often seem wildly out of control but their crews have special techniques.

*Right Below*
This well-organised crew is demonstrating a classic technique for righting a capsized boat. They have manoeuvred head to wind, fully pulled down the centreboard and are standing on it, levering their combined weight against the rig. Once upright and under way the venturi drainers (note dark patch) will soon clear the hull of water. Sydney Morning Herald

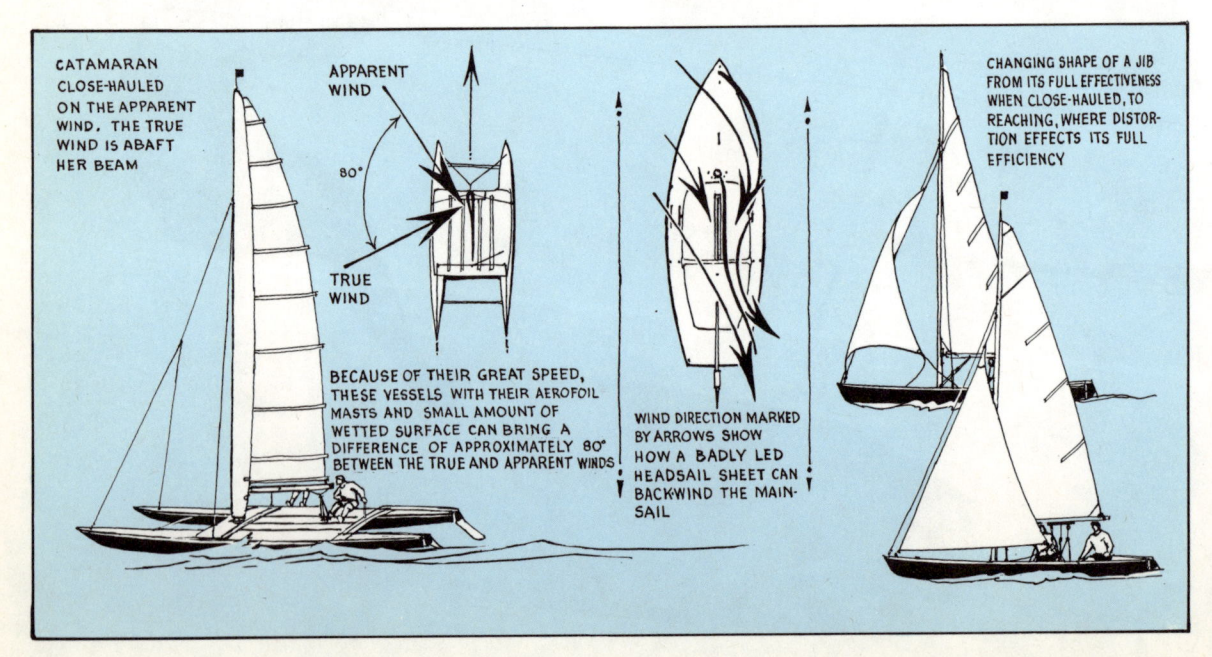

CATAMARAN CLOSE-HAULED ON THE APPARENT WIND. THE TRUE WIND IS ABAFT HER BEAM

APPARENT WIND

80°

TRUE WIND

BECAUSE OF THEIR GREAT SPEED, THESE VESSELS WITH THEIR AEROFOIL MASTS AND SMALL AMOUNT OF WETTED SURFACE CAN BRING A DIFFERENCE OF APPROXIMATELY 80° BETWEEN THE TRUE AND APPARENT WINDS

WIND DIRECTION MARKED BY ARROWS SHOW HOW A BADLY LED HEADSAIL SHEET CAN BACKWIND THE MAINSAIL

CHANGING SHAPE OF A JIB FROM ITS FULL EFFECTIVENESS WHEN CLOSE-HAULED, TO REACHING, WHERE DISTORTION EFFECTS ITS FULL EFFICIENCY

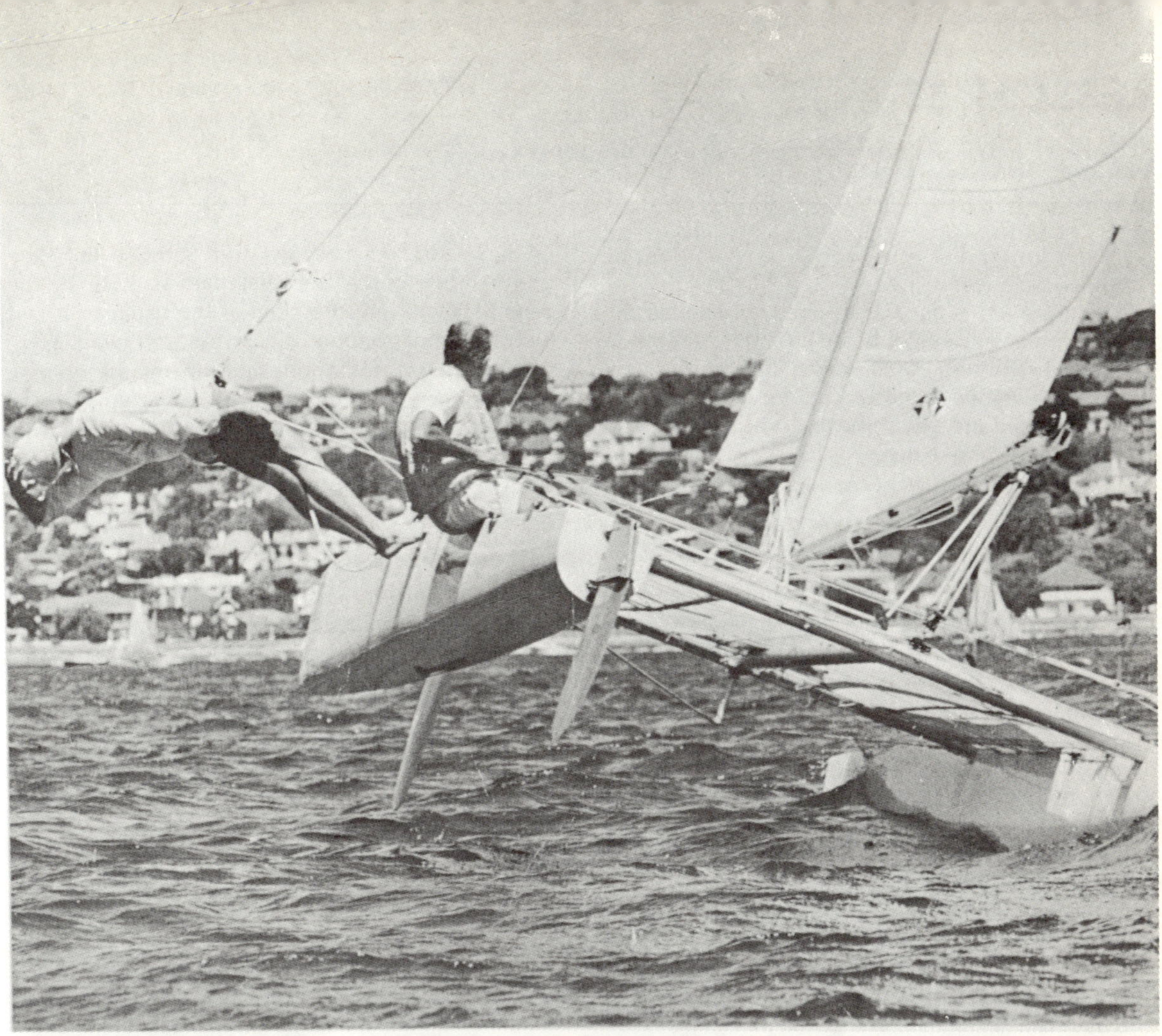

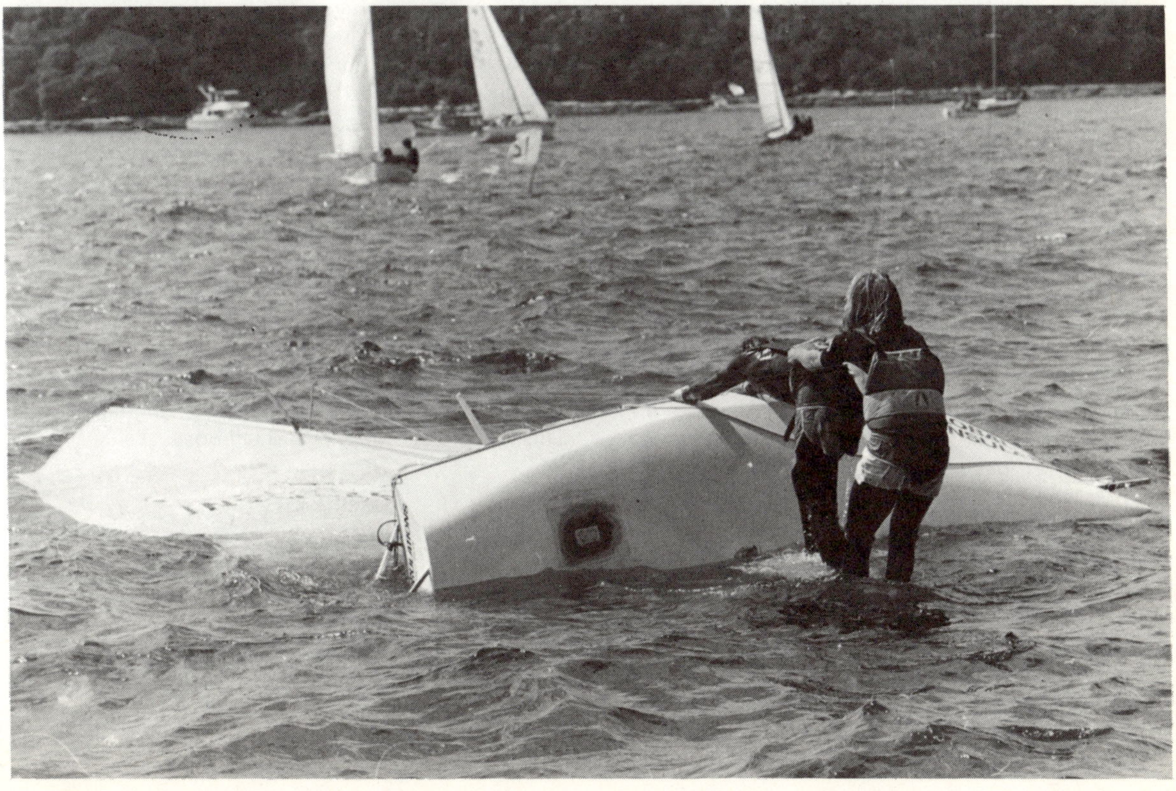

# LESSON 31
# Overlapping headsails

Various forms of jibs have been evolved and can be classified into definite categories.

The 'pure' jib is one which does not overlap the mast; on many classes of boats jibs are restricted to this shape only because there is a limit on the total sail area permitted. However, if a boat is granted a liberal sail area and is of a type that is hard to keep on an even keel in a fresh breeze, such as a Flying Dutchman, it is then beneficial to overlap the mast with a headsail.

Overlapping headsails are called genoa jibs because the first boats to use them were international 6-metre class yachts racing at a regatta in Genoa, Italy. The rules of the class did not call for measurement of the overlap of the headsail and thus the genoa started off as a rule cheater. Theoreticians and practical yachtsmen already knew that overlapping headsails had many advantages over pure jibs in some conditions, and the famous old Sydney yacht, *Brothers,* still sailing on the Harbour in 1981, is credited with having carried Australia's first genoa jib in 1908.

One of the biggest advantages of genoa jibs is that boats built to carry them, with mainsails to suit, tend to have two almost identical centres of sail area, in other words, the centres of effort of the sails are close together. The two sails are almost equal in area. Thus, when a boat is over-powered or the wind fluctuates, the mainsail on a boat with a genoa jib can be eased off and trimmed on without altering the reaction on the helm very much. But this system cannot be used so well on a boat with a 'pure' jib; such boats usually have mainsails much larger than their jibs, and the individual centres of area are further apart than on boats with genoa jibs.

In some rigs, such as those on modern One Ton Cup ocean racing type of yachts, the centres of area of the huge genoa and mainsail are so close together that in heavy weather it can pay to lower the mainsail altogether and beat to windward with the genoa only: the advantage is that it can save the boat from carrying a virtually useless mainsail flapping from its mast.

An interesting and once very popular type of jib is the so-called yankee jib, a very high-cut, narrow sail, with its sheets necessarily led well aft in the boat. It is a good type of sail for a cruising boat but for a long time has been out of fashion on racing boats that can conveniently carry genoa jibs. A yankee jib was used with success as a heavy weather sail on the Admiral's Cup yacht, *Ragamuffin,* and is still popular for close reaching on some offshore boats.

On big vessels it can be combined with a genoa staysail to provide two areas of sail more easily handled than one giant genoa running into 90 square metres or more. Although use of a yankee jib splits up the headsail area it is awkward to tack with. There is not much space between the headstay of the genoa staysail and the clew of the yankee jib and they are prone to foul.

Nevertheless, for a long time it was the opinion of some people that a yankee jib and a genoa staysail provided a headsail rig superior to a full genoa even for moderately-sized yachts—these days that argument has little justification.

Yankee jibs rightly earned support some years ago when sailcloth and sailmaking technology were not at as high a standard as they are today. Genoa jibs then were difficult to make and would not hold their shape because of their great size and the demands that they made on the structural strength of sailcloth. Thus they were indeed inferior to combinations of smaller genoa staysails and smaller yankee headsails that could be made to hold their shape.

In addition, some years ago headsail sheet winches were not as efficient as they are today and genoas could not be sheeted in correctly. But now, with strong, stable cloth made of synthetic fibres, and highly efficient winches, the full-size genoa can be made to hold its shape and can be sheeted in efficiently.

Although the genoa has been proved a much superior sail aerodynamically (theoretically and in practice) to the yankee jib and genoa staysail combination, one must concede that the yankee jib, because its clew is so high, is superior to a genoa when a boat is reaching. The yankee can be sheeted to keep a good shape and exhaust the wind better on a reach, but the genoa, when eased, twists its leech badly, hooks back inboard and does not exhaust the wind properly. However, these days, when reaching across the breeze, we can carry properly-cut spinnakers of modern, synthetic cloth, eliminating the need for genoas for this angle of sailing.

So the argument for yankee jibs overall is not really valid.

Other types of headsails are used for special boats and special purposes and have some fancy names, among them quadrilateral staysails, spinnaker staysails, ghosters, bloopers and tall boys.

| | | |
|---|---|---|
| SAILING TO WINDWARD UNDER GENOA ONLY | |  THE DIFFERENCE BETWEEN A YAWL AND A KETCH IS GENERALLY DETERMINED BY THIS RULE — IF THE MIZZENMAST IS STEPPED AFT OF THE RUDDER POST, THE VESSEL IS A YAWL, AND IF STEPPED FORARD SHE IS KETCH RIGGED |
| MASTHEAD SLOOP UNDER OVERLAPPING GENOA. LEECH IS CUT HOLLOW | KETCH UNDER DOUBLE CLEWED GHOSTER, MAIN, MIZZEN STAYSAIL AND MIZZEN | YAWL UNDER SPINNAKER AND CHEATER OR SPINNAKER STAYSAIL. SHE IS ALSO CARRYING A MIZZEN STAYSAIL |
| STAYSAIL SCHOONER UNDER HER FOUR LOWERS, JIB, FORE STAYSAIL, MAIN STAYSAIL AND MAIN. SHE IS ALSO CARRYING A FISHERMAN STAYSAIL | MASTHEAD SLOOP HOVE-TO UNDER SPITFIRE JIB AND STORM TRYSAIL | BERMUDA CUTTER UNDER MAIN, GENOA AND YANKEE JIB |
| SLOOP WITH THREE QUARTER RIG | 30 SQUARE METRE RACING SLOOP | OLD STYLE GAFF CUTTER. SHE IS CARRYING A JACK YARD TOPSAIL AND HAS HER JIB TOPSAIL IN STOPS |

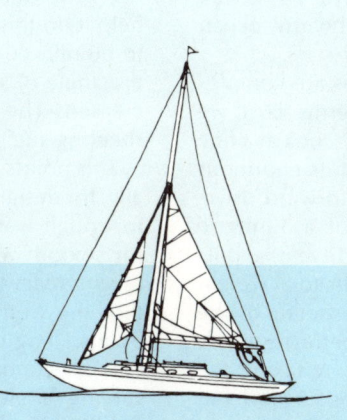

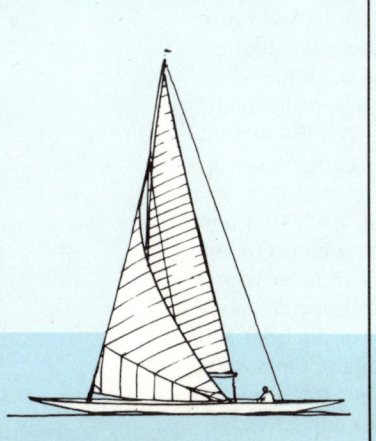

# LESSON 32
# Setting up headsails

Control of the headsail can be achieved in three ways:
- the first is by adjusting its attitude, or angle, to the centreline of the boat;
- the second is by adjusting its shape or draught;
- the third is by adjusting its trim with the sheet.

The first adjustment is decided, more or less arbitrarily, when the boat is being built and the mast stepped and rigged, so there is little chance of adjustment when sailing. Still, before you get under way it is as well to see if the attitude of the jib to the centreline is correct. You should examine the angle of the jib sheeting position athwartships compared with the centreline of the boat, an angle which will vary according to the type of boat, e.g. a 12-metre class yacht, with a waterline length of 14m and a beam of 3.65m, normally should have its genoa jib sheeted at an angle of about 8 degrees from the centreline, measured from the tack fastening; a Flying Dutchman of 6.09m should have its genoa sheeted at about 12 degrees, and a beamy ocean racer at about 15 degrees.

The reasons for these sheeting angles are complex but we may consider them in simple terms. First, we must keep in mind that sheeting in the genoa at a fine angle to the wind, as for a 12-metre, puts enormous side force on the hull and not much forward drive. But the narrow, fine-sectioned hull of a 12-metre does not need much forward force to drive it, and its high ballast ratio (about 70 per cent of its total weight is in its ballast keel) resists heeling forces set up by the side load. The result is that the 12-metre responds quickly to the narrow sheeting angle by taking the least line of resistance—that is, it moves forward and sails close to the wind.

We might compare this response to narrow sheeting with the behaviour of a car travelling on a flat road in top gear. Easily driven boats, either because of their shape or because of their high ballast ratio, move into top gear very easily. Slower boats that do not have such finely-driven hulls and such high ballast resistance to side forces—and especially boats sailing in rough water—need to be given the benefit of low gear. They need coarse sheeting angles, say up to 15 degrees.

We must use our own judgement, on a trial and error basis, for types of boats in between. For example, say we have a full-bodied ocean racer with a high ballast ratio. The high ballast ratio indicates a fine angle of sheeting, and the beam of the boat and the rough sea conditions a coarse angle. On such a boat we should have a headsail sheet track on the outer edge of the deck for a rough sea and a headsail sheet track set inboard for light weather and a smooth sea. Care should also be taken to see that the chain plates of such a boat are set inboard enough and that the rigging spreaders are short enough to allow correct sheeting of the genoa on the inner track; in other words, that the genoa, when sheeted in, does not press against the spreaders and against the lower shrouds.

To understand the reason for a coarse angle of headsail sheeting in a heavy sea or on an unstable boat with a low ballast ratio, one must remember the following points.

When a boat is on a wind the keel is like a hydrofoil or an aeroplane wing and is just as important as the sail.

In smooth water the keel can easily do its job of resisting side forces.

In a seaway the keel is subjected to sudden increases of side load as the boat slams into waves. Hence a stiffer boat, that is, one of high ballast ratio, operates at a reasonably upright attitude and gives the keel a better set of conditions to work under. To help it do this the side load imposed by the jib needs to be relaxed a little; in other words, in rough water the angle of sheeting to the centreline should be increased. The less stable the boat, the coarser the sheeting angle should be.

This points to an interesting proposition, theoretically, for designers, namely: should not boats designed for rough water have larger keel profiles than those for smooth water? In fact there has been a trend in recent years to reduce the size of keel profiles and thus the wetted surface and to compensate for this by installing on the after ends of keels special 'trim tabs' (secondary rudders) which may be locked at varying angles to prevent the loss of directional stability. There is still room for argument about their value, and keel shape remains one of the fields where the greatest advancement is to be made in yacht design.

RUDDER
TRIM-TAB

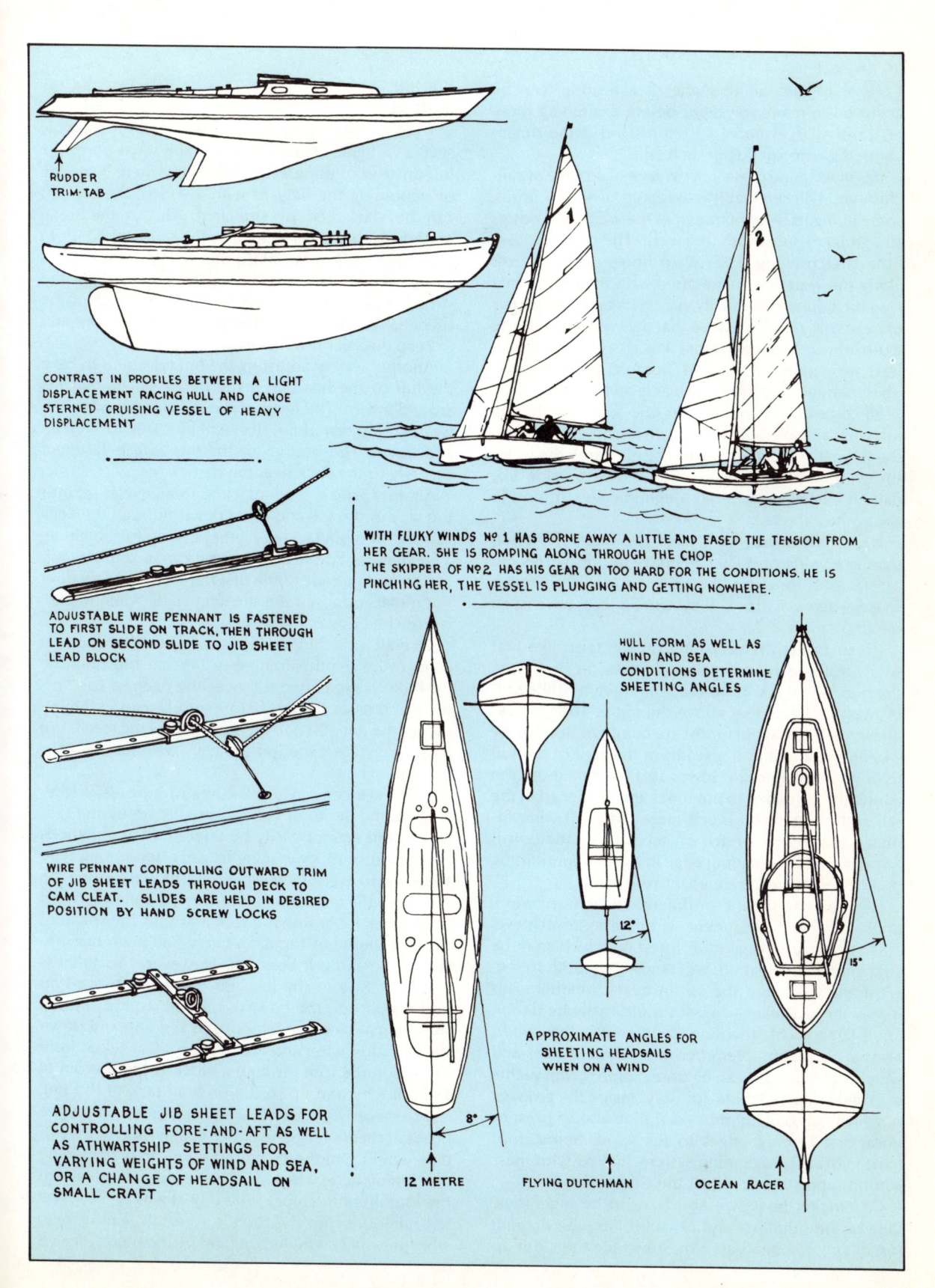

CONTRAST IN PROFILES BETWEEN A LIGHT DISPLACEMENT RACING HULL AND CANOE STERNED CRUISING VESSEL OF HEAVY DISPLACEMENT

ADJUSTABLE WIRE PENNANT IS FASTENED TO FIRST SLIDE ON TRACK, THEN THROUGH LEAD ON SECOND SLIDE TO JIB SHEET LEAD BLOCK

WIRE PENNANT CONTROLLING OUTWARD TRIM OF JIB SHEET LEADS THROUGH DECK TO CAM CLEAT. SLIDES ARE HELD IN DESIRED POSITION BY HAND SCREW LOCKS

ADJUSTABLE JIB SHEET LEADS FOR CONTROLLING FORE-AND-AFT AS WELL AS ATHWARTSHIP SETTINGS FOR VARYING WEIGHTS OF WIND AND SEA, OR A CHANGE OF HEADSAIL ON SMALL CRAFT

WITH FLUKY WINDS N° 1 HAS BORNE AWAY A LITTLE AND EASED THE TENSION FROM HER GEAR. SHE IS ROMPING ALONG THROUGH THE CHOP.
THE SKIPPER OF N°2 HAS HIS GEAR ON TOO HARD FOR THE CONDITIONS. HE IS PINCHING HER, THE VESSEL IS PLUNGING AND GETTING NOWHERE.

HULL FORM AS WELL AS WIND AND SEA CONDITIONS DETERMINE SHEETING ANGLES

APPROXIMATE ANGLES FOR SHEETING HEADSAILS WHEN ON A WIND

12 METRE — 8°
FLYING DUTCHMAN — 12°
OCEAN RACER — 15°

# LESSON 33
## Shape of headsails

Control of the sailing shape of a headsail can be achieved in many ways, but before examining these methods it is essential to understand some details about the construction of such sails.

If you examine closely the weave of a piece of sailcloth you will see that it is made up of sets of fibres, some along its length (known as the warp) and others straight across its width (the weft). The cloth has very little stretch along these warp fibres and even less along the weft fibres compared with the stretch that may be induced diagonally, across its bias. The panels in headsails are arranged so that the weft fibres of the cloth (those that run across the weave and stretch less) are parallel to the foot. Because a jib or genoa jib is triangular in shape, the bias is on the luff.

Since headsails are held on one side only, by the luff wire, and are free-standing on the other two sides, there is a lot of load on them. The bias stretches when the wind applies pressure, and allows a shape like half an ellipse, considered longitudinally, to form in the body of the sail.

High, narrow headsails have less bias on the luff than low, wide ones, like genoas, but this works out satisfactorily because they do not need so much shape—being narrow, they should not have such depth of 'drive'.

When the sail is very long on the foot, like that used on 30 square metre class yachts or on 12-metres, the bias below the mitre (or central seam of the sail) is much less than that above the mitre. Then we get uneven stretch, which must be compensated for by 'swelling' (tapering) the seams in the foot of the sail to build shape into this lower area. This method also allows the sailmaker to put the shape further aft in the sail and to control it much more than if it were induced entirely by stretch on the luff. In addition it imparts a shallow leading edge in a genoa, permitting its angle of attack to be high into the wind.

Headsail adjustment for different weights of wind, unlike mainsail adjustment, is not easy to achieve. This is largely because the forestay, which may be straight in light weather, will tend to sag both to leeward and back into the sail in heavy weather. This makes the sail fuller when it should really be flatter. On a large yacht, adapting to different wind conditions is no real problem because different sizes and weights of headsails can be used. Some racing yachts use rigid hollowed metal forestays inside the grooves of which headsail luff ropes can slide and so present unsagging leading edges to the wind. Some, too, have hydraulic tensioning systems linked with mast shrouds and stays to adjust the shape of sails.

On smaller boats we also have to be ingenious. One of the simplest ways of controlling the draught (or 'drive') of a headsail is by stretching the cloth up the luff, which moves the deepest part of the sail forward.

This can be achieved by having an elastic material such as a light terylene rope or tape sewn on to the luff (instead of using a rigid luff wire); then, by easing or tightening the halyard with a winch, the sail luff can be slackened or stretched. This is the usual method with a boat which has the sail hanked on to a permanent forestay. With this system, as the luff is stretched the clew of the sail rises and, since the stretching is done in heavy weather, the lead of the sheet has to be moved aft to compensate for this and to keep the sail drawing properly.

Another way of adjusting the luff tension is to have the luff of the headsail made into a sleeve that fits around a wire. The head of the sail is fastened to the wire but the rest of the sleeved luff is free to slide up and down. The bottom of the luff wire is fastened securely to the deck near the stem.

Another wire is then attached to an eyelet let into the tack of the sail and is led down through the deck to an adjustable tackle or other device for obtaining a mechanical advantage. When it can be applied, this method is superior to the first because the clew does not move and upset the sheeting angle when the sail is stretched down.

Overall, stretching of the luff of a headsail does not change the depth of curve in the sail but only the position of the curve; it moves the deepest part forward and eases the leech. Conversely, easing the luff moves the deepest part aft and tightens the leech. We therefore stretch the luff in heavy weather and ease it out in light.

While we can move the curve of a headsail fore-and-aft, the depth of curve is usually set by the sailmaker and cannot easily be altered. Many methods have been tried, one being to use a tensioning wire led from an eye set a few centimetres back along the foot from the tack. When this eye was pulled forward to the tack it *became* the tack and thus the shape of the sail altered as though a curve had been put into the luff, making it very full. However, this fullness was too close to the luff and had to be moved aft and higher into the body of the sail. To move it aft, the original tack was let loose to slide up and down the sail's luff wire, and another wire was taken from the eye in the foot through a block at the bottom of the luff wire and up to the original tack of the sail.

The *theory* was that as the sail was eased off (by the headsail sheet) in light weather, the tension of the luff tape would pull the tack up the luff, thus tightening the joining wire, which in turn would pull the eye in the foot up to the block. The object was to make the sail fuller and put the drive further aft. Conversely, when the sail was pulled on hard by the sheet, the eye

64

in the foot would move away from the tack, making the sail flat; this also tightened the wire and, by pulling the luff down, stretched it and put the drive up close to the front of the sail.

So much for the theory. The big problem, *in practice,* with this experimental system was to decide the right degree of tension for various weights of wind without constant adjustments, and to overcome friction, which was considerable. So the experiments, by amateur and professional sailmakers and boat tuners, go on.

Probably the most practical way of getting a little change in the depth of curve in a headsail is to change the luff and leech tensions—by easing and tightening the jib halyard and moving the position of the sheet lead forward and aft. This is largely a matter of trial and error for each individual sail. It's easy enough to ease and tighten the tension on the jib halyard to get a variety of adjustments, but to make much change in the sheet lead angle it is necessary to have the clew of the sail close to the lead block which you move forward or aft. If the clew is a metre or so away you might have to move the lead block 15 cm to get much change in leech tension. To get sheet lead blocks nearer to the clews of their headsails, providing more potential adjustment of leech tension, many shrewd skippers have jib sheet lead tracks built up from deck level.

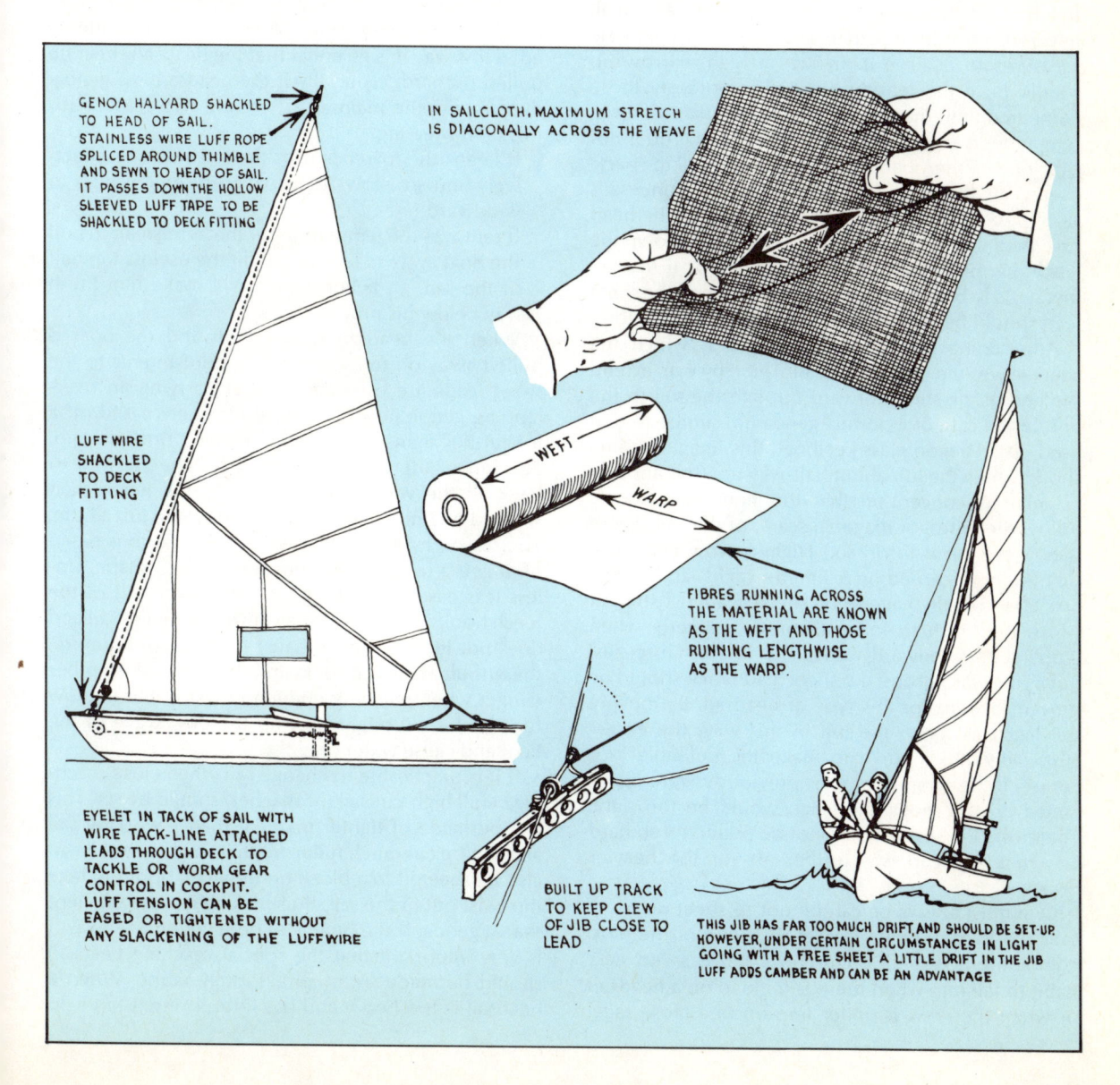

GENOA HALYARD SHACKLED TO HEAD OF SAIL. STAINLESS WIRE LUFF ROPE SPLICED AROUND THIMBLE AND SEWN TO HEAD OF SAIL. IT PASSES DOWN THE HOLLOW SLEEVED LUFF TAPE TO BE SHACKLED TO DECK FITTING

IN SAILCLOTH, MAXIMUM STRETCH IS DIAGONALLY ACROSS THE WEAVE

LUFF WIRE SHACKLED TO DECK FITTING

WEFT

WARP

FIBRES RUNNING ACROSS THE MATERIAL ARE KNOWN AS THE WEFT AND THOSE RUNNING LENGTHWISE AS THE WARP.

EYELET IN TACK OF SAIL WITH WIRE TACK-LINE ATTACHED LEADS THROUGH DECK TO TACKLE OR WORM GEAR CONTROL IN COCKPIT. LUFF TENSION CAN BE EASED OR TIGHTENED WITHOUT ANY SLACKENING OF THE LUFFWIRE

BUILT UP TRACK TO KEEP CLEW OF JIB CLOSE TO LEAD

THIS JIB HAS FAR TOO MUCH DRIFT, AND SHOULD BE SET-UP. HOWEVER, UNDER CERTAIN CIRCUMSTANCES IN LIGHT GOING WITH A FREE SHEET A LITTLE DRIFT IN THE JIB LUFF ADDS CAMBER AND CAN BE AN ADVANTAGE

# LESSON 34
## Trimming headsails

Until now we have considered the set curves in headsails and how to control them. Trimming a headsail to suit a particular weight of wind is another matter. We know we can change the whole shape of a headsail dramatically by moving the sheet lead forward or aft, inboard or outboard, by easing it off and hauling it on. The big question always is: how tight the foot and the leech of the sail should be to suit a given condition of wind or a particular course.

First, let us deal with windward sailing in a moderate weight of breeze. We should study the type of sail we are using—it is no use making one hard and fast rule for all types of headsails.

One popular misconception many yachtsmen seem to have is that the tension on the foot and leech of all headsails must be exactly even. Some go to extreme measures to achieve it. In fact, a high, narrow jib should have the tension along the foot very loose compared with that on the leech. The main thing to remember is that in a weight of breeze that does not over-power the boat, the sail should start to 'back' evenly all the way down the luff when one sails slowly up into the wind. If the sail backs at the head first, then it should be sheeted more tightly down the leech, by moving the sheet lead forward; if the sail first starts to back low down on the luff, then the sheet lead should be moved further aft to tighten the foot.

After doing this, check the angle at which the sheet leaves the clew of the sail. Then, by eye, extend the line of the sheet forward through the sail to the luff. In the case of a normal genoa jib, similar to that used on a Dragon class keelboat, this imaginary line should strike the luff about half-way up. (It is another popular misconception that this line must exactly follow the mitre, or diagonal seam, of the sail. There is no need for it to do so.) High, narrow headsails, such as those carried on 5.5-metre yachts and on the Star class, usually have to be sheeted almost straight down the leech to make them set properly when working to windward, especially in fresh breezes. But as the wind drops, the sheet lead block should be moved forward for this type of headsail. By moving the leech closer to the luff in this way, the excess cloth falls into a curve to make the sail fuller. Of course, if the same tension as previously were maintained on the sheet, the leech would be too tight. Therefore, the sheet should not be pulled on so hard as when the lead was further aft for the heavier breeze.

One must always be careful not to sheet on headsails too hard in light weather. It is one of the most common errors of all yacht crews and is a very easy habit to fall into when there is no load on a headsail or when the crew is under tension in a close race.

Sometimes you will find that by easing the jib only a slight amount in light weather you will open the gap (or slot) between the mainsail and the headsail and start a flow of air that will suck the boat along. When the jib is pulled on too hard it constricts the gap between mainsail and headsail and stops air passing freely between them, with the result that the jib becomes little more than a brake on the boat.

As a general rule, in heavy weather the headsail sheet lead should be moved aft. By this means the top of the sail will be allowed to lie off to leeward and only the bottom half of the sail will be drawing hard. This system lowers the point of pressure on the whole rig, making the boat more stable. It also opens the slot between headsail and mainsail and allows more air to pass between them. When one's gear is adjusted in this way it is essential that the headsail sheet be pulled on hard, especially if the headsail is a genoa, overlapping the mainsail. There are two reasons for this tight sheeting.

It keeps the lower part of the sail working effectively and so allows the boat to be sailed high to windward.

It removes the temptation for the helmsman to pull the boat away to leeward to fill the useless top half of the sail, an action which will make him finish way below his proper course.

When the headsail is eased off and the boat is pulled away on to a close reach, adjustments to the sheet leads are essential. A boat carrying an overlapping genoa jib should have the sheet eased off a lot further than one carrying a small, orthodox jib. The luff of the genoa should at first be allowed to back all the way from the tack to the head, then sheeted on only slightly, still allowing it to luff a little. The reason for this is that when a genoa jib is eased off it gets a lot of curve in its fore-and-aft shape. Unless it is eased off a *long way* the lower half of the leech hooks back across the centre line of the sail and does not let the wind exhaust from it. Furthermore, the turbulent air will backwind the mainsail. Another danger when reaching under a genoa is that the low foot of the sail might pick up the bow wave of the boat and cause water drag.

If it is practicable to change sail when close reaching, a full high-cut sail (or **reacher**) should be set. This can be made of lighter material than a working sail and can be cut much fuller. With its higher foot it can also be sheeted to a block on the main boom to take the twist out of the sail, thus making it more efficient than a genoa. If the boat is to be sailed in a seaway it is very important that the special reaching headsail should be made from light, springy fabric. When a headsail is too heavy and has little spring it tends to thrash back and forth every time the boat hits a wave and slows up; but a springy sail, because of its stretch, will keep drawing and continue to pull the boat along through the wave. Do not discount this effect as an unnecessary refinement, as the difference can be considerable. A heavy, unyielding headsail transmits a fluctuating, jerky power to the boat. A light, springy one provides a smooth, constant force.

When close reaching, boats with small jibs, such as 5.5-metres or Star class yachts, should have a headsail sheet lead outboard of the normal lead for working to windward. This outer lead block can have its own sheet set up in it permanently, with a snap shackle or clip on it to attach to the clew of the jib when the sail needs to be eased. The snap shackle can be clipped on to the sail in a few seconds and the load transferred from the permanent 'working' sheet to the reaching sheet. I have seen such a seemingly minor technique increase a yacht's speed by half a knot in a moderate breeze.

If a headsail is built with an adjustable or stretchy luff this should be eased when close reaching, to make the sail fuller. The most important thing to remember when trimming a headsail for close reaching is to adjust the headsail and mainsail sheets so that the boat has neutral helm.

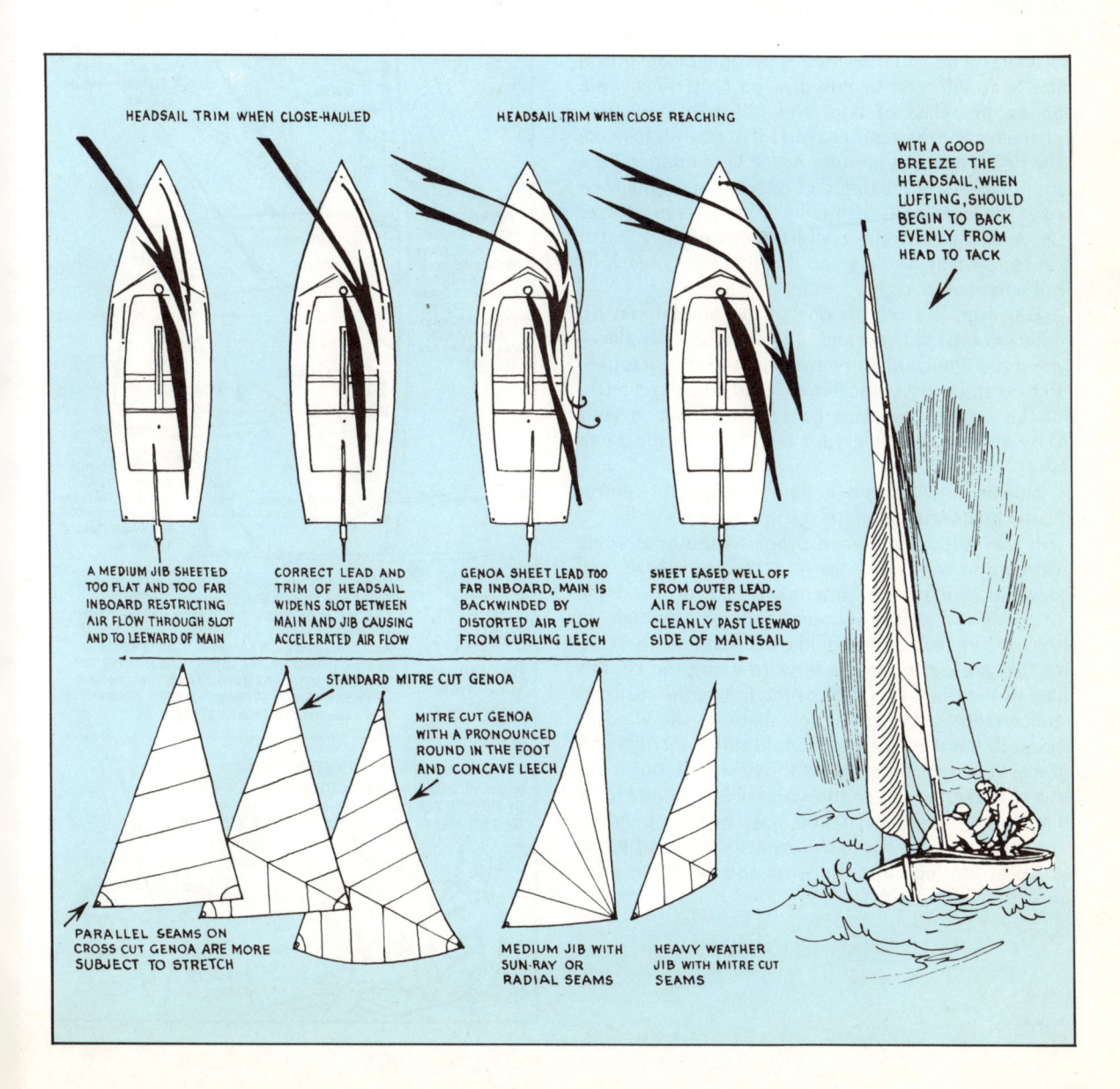

HEADSAIL TRIM WHEN CLOSE-HAULED

HEADSAIL TRIM WHEN CLOSE REACHING

WITH A GOOD BREEZE THE HEADSAIL, WHEN LUFFING, SHOULD BEGIN TO BACK EVENLY FROM HEAD TO TACK

A MEDIUM JIB SHEETED TOO FLAT AND TOO FAR INBOARD RESTRICTING AIR FLOW THROUGH SLOT AND TO LEEWARD OF MAIN

CORRECT LEAD AND TRIM OF HEADSAIL WIDENS SLOT BETWEEN MAIN AND JIB CAUSING ACCELERATED AIR FLOW

GENOA SHEET LEAD TOO FAR INBOARD, MAIN IS BACKWINDED BY DISTORTED AIR FLOW FROM CURLING LEECH

SHEET EASED WELL OFF FROM OUTER LEAD. AIR FLOW ESCAPES CLEANLY PAST LEEWARD SIDE OF MAINSAIL

STANDARD MITRE CUT GENOA

MITRE CUT GENOA WITH A PRONOUNCED ROUND IN THE FOOT AND CONCAVE LEECH

PARALLEL SEAMS ON CROSS CUT GENOA ARE MORE SUBJECT TO STRETCH

MEDIUM JIB WITH SUN-RAY OR RADIAL SEAMS

HEAVY WEATHER JIB WITH MITRE CUT SEAMS

# LESSON 35
## Masts

So far in these advanced lessons we have concentrated on the driving force of the boat—the sails. Now that we have a better knowledge of their functions it is time to consider that very important feature of our boat from which the sails are set—the mast. Its position and angle in any boat are the core of good sailing. Too often they are completely ignored.

As a general rule, in most classes of racing boats, the mast should be set up almost vertical with a slight rake aft when the craft is afloat at its normal sailing trim. The only exceptions should be for extreme classes of boats with radical rigs: two such exceptions are boats of traditional Australian design, the racing 18-footer and the 3.5m Vee Jay.

The 18-footer has a very large sail area for its hull displacement, and if its mast is set up almost vertical the boat will tend to nosedive on runs downwind. So on this class of boat and others of the same character, the mast must have a lot of rake aft to make the rig lift the boat on runs. A Vee Jay's mast needs a lot of rake, but for a different reason. Under the class rules the leech of its mainsail is short. If its mast is set up vertically its boom cocks uphill so much that it causes extreme air drag and the boat won't reach its full potential speed.

However, if a boat is one of the normal classes, with a normal sail area and sail shape for its displacement and if the hull is free from built-in vice, it is hard to beat an almost vertical mast. Study the exact angle of the mast of the most consistent winner in your class and try adjusting your own mast in the same way.

Let us now consider Bermuda-rigged, centreboard boats with modern staying systems.

If the sails are designed properly, the boat while working to windward, say in a 12-knot breeze, will travel at its maximum potential speed for this angle of sailing and weight of breeze and point up high. As the wind increases we should try to bend the mast aft, so that the centre moves forward along the centreline of the boat. This flattens the luff of the mainsail and presents a better aerofoil shape to the wind. If properly handled, the boat should still point high and travel at its maximum speed to windward. But there is a critical point: when the mainsail is flattened to its limit by bending the mast and, if we wish, by bending the middle of the boom downwards, the boat tends to point too high into the wind and begins to slow down.

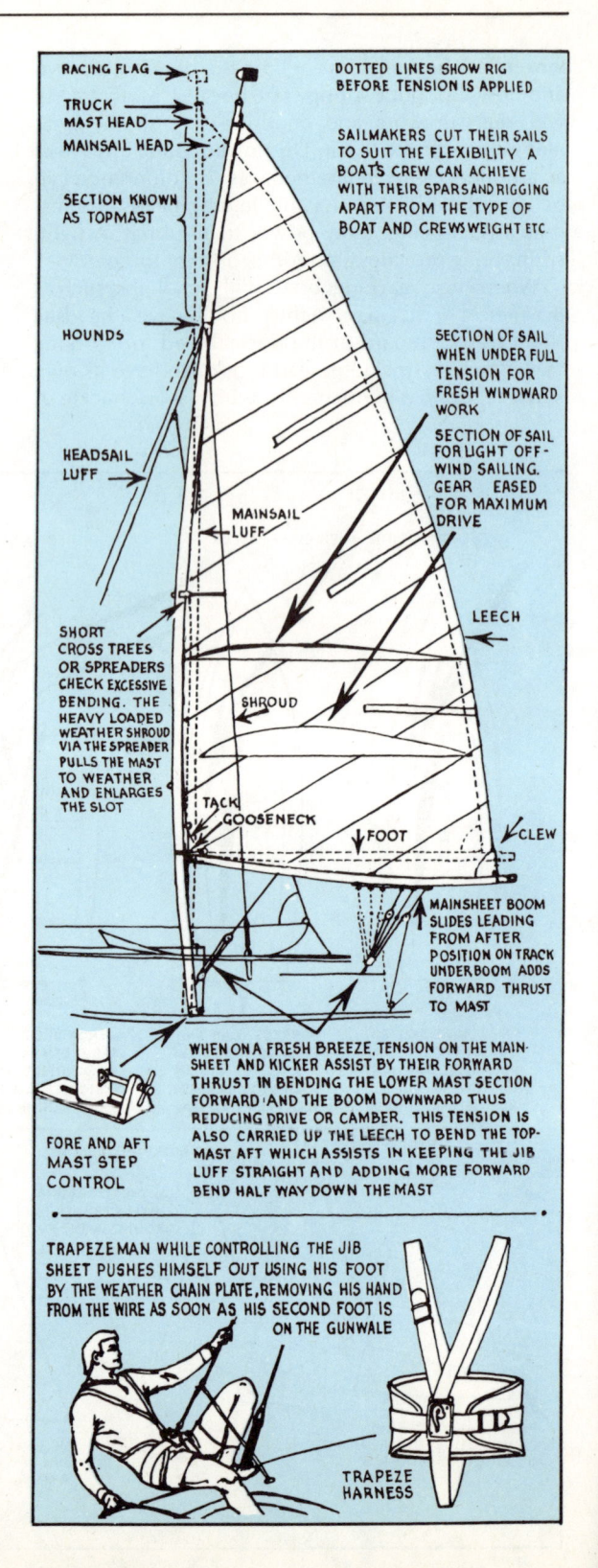

Australian 16-foot skiffs are among the fastest monohull boats their length in the world, especially on shy reaches. They carry a minimum crew of four and restricted sails. Although hull dimensions have changed little in 80 years, the boats are now of lightweight construction with buoyancy tanks bow and stern and easily rightable after a capsize. *Sydney Morning Herald*

# LESSON 36
# Heavy winds

In high winds it may become difficult to stop the boat heeling excessively and capsizing.

There is, however, another alternative. By letting the top section of the mast sag away to leeward, we give the upper part of the mainsail a shape that will drive the boat faster and at the same time open the wind slot between the leeward side of the mainsail and the windward side of the jib. This also will make the boat go faster and will give it more stability. Although it is travelling fast, the boat will not now point so high to windward as previously, so in between the gusts when we want to come up closer to the wind, we need techniques to straighten the fore-and-aft bend and to correct the sag to leeward.

In some types of boats the best way to control the fore-and-aft bend is to have the step of the mast fixed and to use a system of chocks on the fore side of the mast where it enters the deck. When the chocks are removed the middle of the mast will bow forward and the top will bend aft; when the chocks are driven down firmly the mast will straighten along almost its whole length. A refinement of this system is a cam attached to a lever and a winch that provides quick and exact adjustment.

To make the mast sag to leeward it is necessary to slack the side rigging. If the mast is stayed with cap shrouds, these will have to be eased; if, instead, it has diamond shrouds supporting it laterally, these will need to be eased slightly. Organising all this on a Bermuda-rigged centreboard boat without letting the mast carry away altogether is not as hard as it might at first seem.

Of course, some boats are precluded from using chocks and cams because their class rules prohibit stepping their masts through the decks. Best known among these types are Lightweight Sharpies, Herons, Gwen 12s and Cherubs. There are some boats, too, that cannot afford to have large slots in their decks to accommodate chocks or a cam because they cannot deal with the water that comes in through the slots. Nevertheless, fore-and-aft mast control can be achieved on these boats in a number of ways.

One is to use a telescopic rod and tube system. A threaded rod with a knurled nut or similar device for screwing it in and out of the tube is fastened to a footplate on the deck for'ard of the mast. The rod is extended to another plate about 60-90 cm up the fore side of the mast. By shortening this rod with the knurled nut a forward bend can be induced in the mast; by lengthening the rod to its fullest extent the mast can be brought back to its normal straightness.

It is also possible to induce forward bend by using a single strut rod fastened to the fore side of a mast, with a slide on the other end of the rod fitting into a track on the deck. A tackle is necessary to move the rod fore-and-aft on the deck and thus, by exerting or relaxing tension, the mast can be bent forward or straightened. Obviously, one disadvantage of this system is that the deck around the tracked area needs to be very strong because the forces at the point of contact are great.

In boats where deck control is inconvenient because they need to be kept watertight, or on yachts on which the forces needed to bend their masts would have to be much greater than those practicable with the simple rod systems described above, fore-and-aft bend can be induced by moving the foot of the mast along its step and by hydraulic systems controlling the rigging.

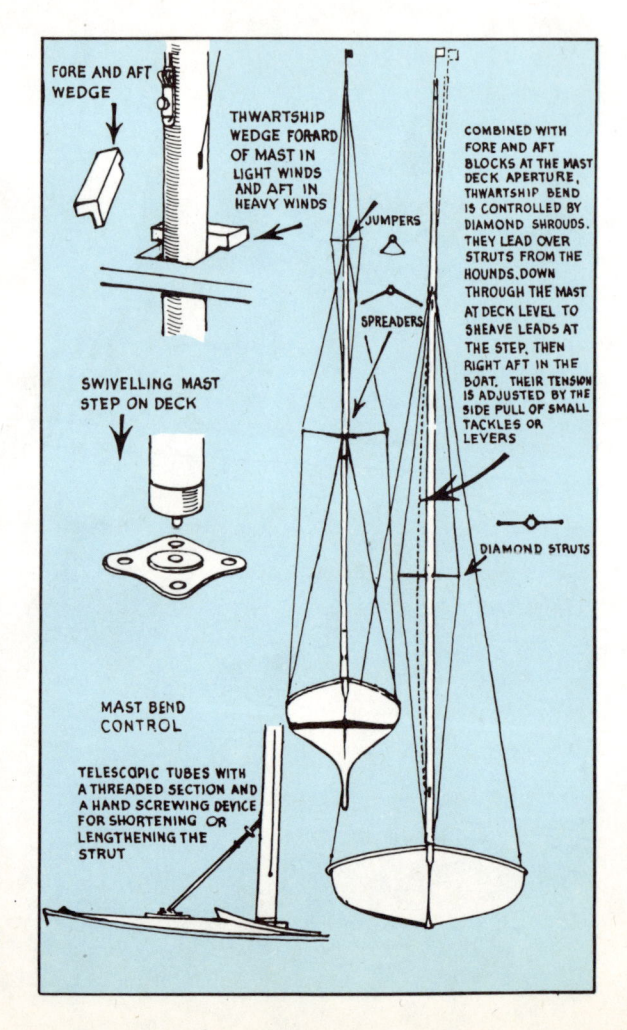

Perfection in shape, rig and skill won the world championship for Australia's 5.5 metre class yacht, *Carabella*, skippered by Olympian David Forbes. Note the spinnaker basket fastened to the shrouds ready for setting as she nears the weather mark, the fold of the mainsail tack induced by the Cunningham Eye tackle, the bend in mast to flatten the sail which is sheeted down hard.

# LESSON 37
# Backstay adjustments

Some big yachts have screw jacks and hydraulic rams built into them for moving their masts along their steps. Since 1964 almost every America's Cup 12-metre class yacht has used a mast ram or a hydraulic tensioning system on the rigging to induce mast bend to suit differing conditions.

Many yachts with topmast backstays, notably the international Soling, Dragon and 5.5-metre classes, have tackles rigged on them for the express purpose of inducing mast bend. (So far I have not detailed the use of this tackle to bend a mast aft, because we have been mainly discussing small centreboard craft which rarely have topmast backstays.) On my own boat, a 7.6m waterline sloop, I have a mechanised worm-drive system with which I can wind in and ease out the topmast backstay tackle. The tackle system especially suits the Dragon class because their compulsory rigging rules require them to have jumper struts on the fore side of their masts, in addition to adjustable running backstays and a topmast backstay. With all these aids, crews can very conveniently ease the jumper struts and sweat up the topmast backstay. This pulls the top of the mast aft and therefore bends the middle forward and flattens the mainsail luff. Similarly, when running before the wind, by easing the topmast backstay tackle many Dragon sailors let the whole mast lean forward and get better downwind performance.

In the case of 5.5-metre class yachts, the topmast backstay and jumper struts are the only rigging to keep the forestay tight, thus allowing the luff of the jib to present a good clean, un-sagging leading edge to the wind when the boat is on a work to windward. The jumper struts need to be set up so that when the backstay is bar tight the mast has the correct heavy weather bend.

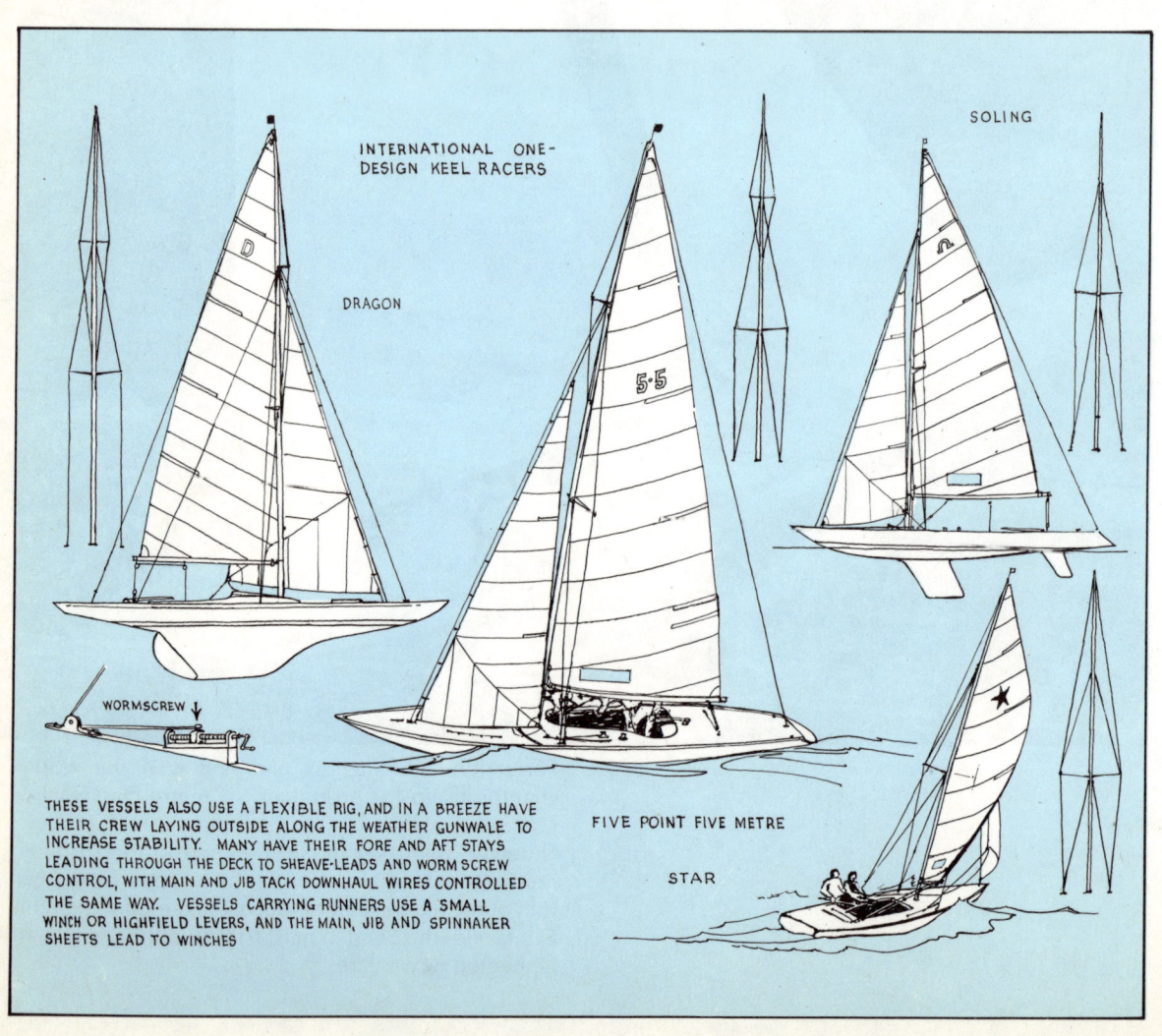

INTERNATIONAL ONE-DESIGN KEEL RACERS

DRAGON

WORMSCREW

THESE VESSELS ALSO USE A FLEXIBLE RIG, AND IN A BREEZE HAVE THEIR CREW LAYING OUTSIDE ALONG THE WEATHER GUNWALE TO INCREASE STABILITY. MANY HAVE THEIR FORE AND AFT STAYS LEADING THROUGH THE DECK TO SHEAVE-LEADS AND WORM SCREW CONTROL, WITH MAIN AND JIB TACK DOWNHAUL WIRES CONTROLLED THE SAME WAY. VESSELS CARRYING RUNNERS USE A SMALL WINCH OR HIGHFIELD LEVERS, AND THE MAIN, JIB AND SPINNAKER SHEETS LEAD TO WINCHES

5·5

FIVE POINT FIVE METRE

SOLING

STAR

Split second co-ordination between helmsman and crew, agility, strength and intelligence are essential for racing an Australian 16 ft skiff, one of the hardest craft in the world to handle and one of the fastest for its length in fresh conditions.

International Dragon class (8.89m) are superb sail carriers and these three are making great pace under shy spinnakers in a fresh breeze. It is the responsibility of the second boat to keep clear of the leader so she is screwing to windward and collapsing her kite. The third yacht is pulling clear under her stern.

# LESSON 38
# Controlling mast bends

In light weather, on a 5.5 or similarly rigged boat, one can afford to ease the backstay to a point where the jib does not sag too much and the inherent elasticity of the mast and the jumper strut wires straighten the mast up to a more suitable light weather curve.

Australia's first Olympic gold medal winner, *Barranjoey*, sailed by Bill Northam, had her mast rigged in this way and her crew, Peter O'Donnell and Dick Sargent, used to adjust the rigging constantly, like piano tuners. They are experts at setting up a mast in any class of boat with just the right tension for the weight of wind. Northam used to disarm his opponents by pretending that he could never get *Barranjoey's* mast exactly right and that O'Donnell and Sargent had to fiddle with it all the time. But he was just as aware as they that a two or three millimetre adjustment in those jumper struts, and a couple of centimetres on the backstay tackle, could make a tremendous improvement in the boat's performance.

Some boats, of course, get fore-and-aft bends in their masts that they could very well do without. Particularly in boats with light masts, these bends can be induced by the force imposed by the angle of the mainsail and the mainboom sheeting. The leech of the mainsail slopes forward and when it is under tension while the boat is working to windward, imparts thrust along the boom and a pull aft on the head of the mast. This puts a considerable but often unrecognised bending load on the mast. It sometimes flattens a mainsail unduly for the weight of wind in which the boat is sailing.

If this is one of your troubles, and you cannot counter or control the mast bend and the consequent flattening of your mainsail, there is another way out. Use a sheeting system so that the blocks on the boom are slightly ahead of the blocks on the mainsheet traveller, or, if you have no mainsheet traveller but lead blocks on the after deck, ahead of these lead blocks. Then, when the sail is hauled on for a work to windward, the sheet will pull aft on the boom and relieve the forward load on the mast. International Star class yachts used to have boom blocks on an adjustable track under the boom for this very purpose.

Few keel yachts are more sensitive to rig adjustments than the international Etchells 22 class 9.14m sloops and, within the limits of the rigid one-design specifications, skippers tune their gear precisely to suit the weight of their crews and the expected strength of wind.

Enormous spinnakers — up to 93 sq.m. in area — are characteristic of 18-footers which have raced in Australia for 90 years and are gradually gaining supporters overseas. Once they were full-bodied boats and needed crews of 15 to balance them. In modern times, with the use of trapezes, they have been refined to lightweight structures with wing frames hinged from side decks and crews of three. They are the world's fastest monohull centreboard boats their length and among the most demanding to sail on and off a wind. *Rudi Sipos*

# LESSON 39
## Side bends

The simplest method of controlling side bend in a mast is that used by international Finn and OK dinghy exponents. Since their boats have no rigging, they have masts made in such a shape and with such a degree of flexibility that they automatically bend sideways to leeward from the top as the wind pressure on their sail increases. It is essential, of course, that there is enough inherent stiffness in such masts to prevent them lying to leeward in light weather. When Finn dinghies were restricted to wooden masts—they are now permitted to have them of aluminium alloy, fibreglass or timber—many skippers started the fashion of 'rigging their boats with a plane', i.e. shaving away just enough of their masts to cause them to bend in hard weather but to stand up in light to moderate winds. But since these Finn and OK dinghies have no rigging they have only limited control of the side bend in their masts. In turbulent water and light winds their performances sometimes suffer through it. As they fall off a sea their masts tend to flick to leeward.

As a general rule, to control bend in a normally rigged small boat it is preferable to have below the hounds a set of diamond stays that can be eased to induce bend in heavy weather. These must of course be adjustable while sailing, to provide for changes in wind strength.

The diamond stays can be of very light wire, since they do not have a great deal of load on them, being intended purely as mast benders and straighteners and not as supports for the mast. But they should be of 1 x 19 strand stainless steel, because this has a minimum of stretch and we wish to keep the system under control. Some helmsmen object to using diamond stays because they can cause difficulties when spinnakers are being hoisted or lowered.

On out-and-out racing yachts, such as Dragons and 5.5-metres, cap shrouds can be made adjustable by means of very small cams fitted on the chain plates. They need a scope of only about a centimetre, which is just enough to let the windward cap shroud slacken as the wind increases and so let the top half of the mast lie off to leeward.

On Dragons and 5.5-metres side play of masts where they enter the deck should also be adjustable. This may be achieved by use of a chock that can be removed in heavy weather. Another way is to have the hole in the deck in the shape of an ellipse, with the wider part forward and the narrower part aft. When the middle of the mast is bent forward in heavy weather to flatten the draught in the sail, the section of the mast going through the deck will move automatically up to windward into the wider part of the hole, bending the top of the mast to leeward. Conversely, when the mast is straightened up for light weather (by the use of forward deck chocks or a cam), the mast will move back into the narrower part of the hole and will *not* tend to lie to leeward.

These devices may seem extreme for the average amateur yachtsman but they are the developments that champions have used to make their boats go faster.

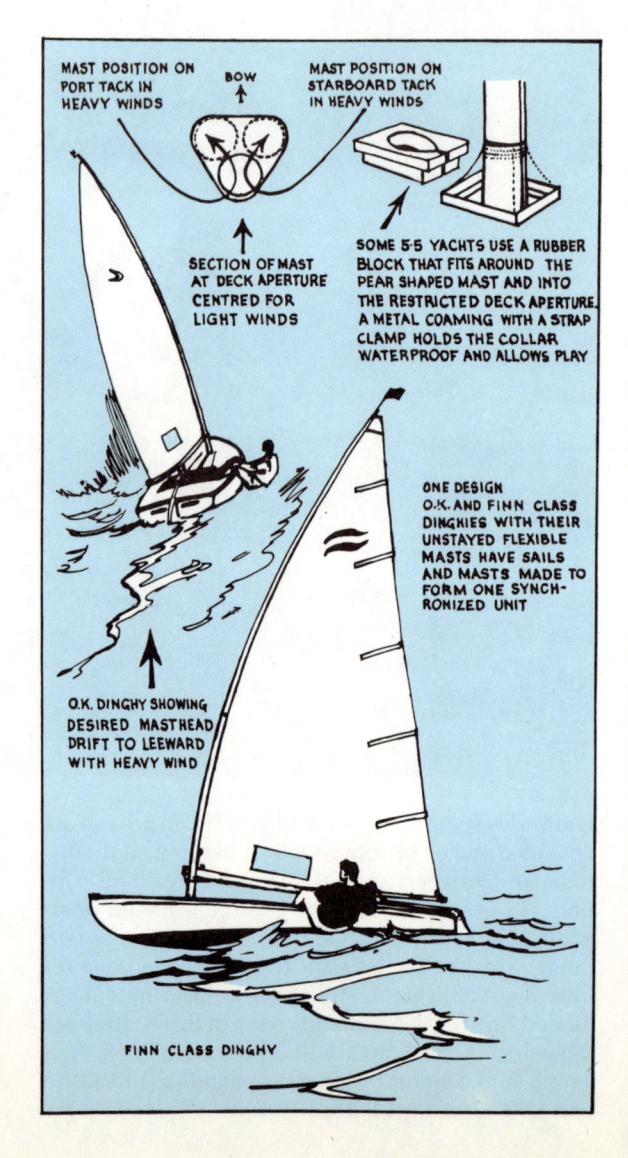

At the weather mark, in close company, helmsmen and crews must judge speed, distance instantaneously and their rights under racing rules. In this world 5.5 metre title race, Sweden's S50 has a narrow lead over Norway's N32 which is shooting up to windward, while Australia's KA25 is slicing under the bows of Australia's KA91. In seconds they'll have spinnakers flying.

# LESSON 40
## Mast shapes

In discussing the use of controlled bends in a mast to improve performance we have pre-supposed that the boat was otherwise sailing at its top potential. It is possible, of course, that the mast you are using is not of the right shape or size, so let us look at that aspect.

No mast one sets out to bend should be pear-shaped unless the class rules make it so, or unless it is possible to revolve the mast in its step to present its leading edge to the wind, or unless the boat carrying it is extremely close-winded and very fast. Revolving masts can be of elongated section so that they become a long narrow aerofoil, like those now used on the C class catamarans. These are ideal, but they are most complicated pieces of engineering and cost almost as much as the rest of the boat. Pear-shaped and elliptical-shaped bendy masts that don't revolve are suitable only for very close-winded boats, like 12-metres, because these boats move so quickly in light airs that the apparent wind is only about 10 degrees off their bows, so that the leading edge of the mast almost points at the wind.

For all practical purposes on ordinary yachts and small boats that rarely sail higher than 45 degrees to the wind, a round bendy mast with as small a diameter as possible, strong walls and adjustable rigging, is preferable. There are two reasons for this. One is that when a round mast bends, it distributes the compression load over a much wider area than does a pear-shaped mast; the other is that a round mast presents an even profile at different angles of attack to the wind and thus reduces air drag. That is to say, on a reach, with the wind abeam, the air drag on a round mast will be considerably less than that on a broad, pear-shaped mast which does not revolve. The round mast, strength for weight, at every angle of bend, is also a better proposition than the pear-shaped mast and can be tapered at the top much more finely in order to reduce weight and air resistance. (Never forget that the less weight you carry aloft the more stable your boat will be.) So the smaller the area of your mast, within reason, in front of your mainsail, the less air drag, the less air turbulence and the greater the efficiency of the mainsail.

During wind tunnel tests for the design of 12-metre masts for the America's Cup, it was found that even normally tapered pear-shaped masts reduced the efficiency of the mainsail for 50 cms aft of the whole length of the luff. This, in effect, was giving away much of the driving force of more than 9 square metres of the 12-metre's mainsail. When there can be such an effect on a boat so close-winded as a 12-metre, it is easy to understand how much more serious air turbulence around a mast can be on less efficient craft. Unfortunately, some yachtsmen—and some designers who should know better—seeing pear-shaped masts and elliptical-shaped masts used on close-winded racing machines, have presumed that they must be the best and have made them fashionable for all sorts of boats.

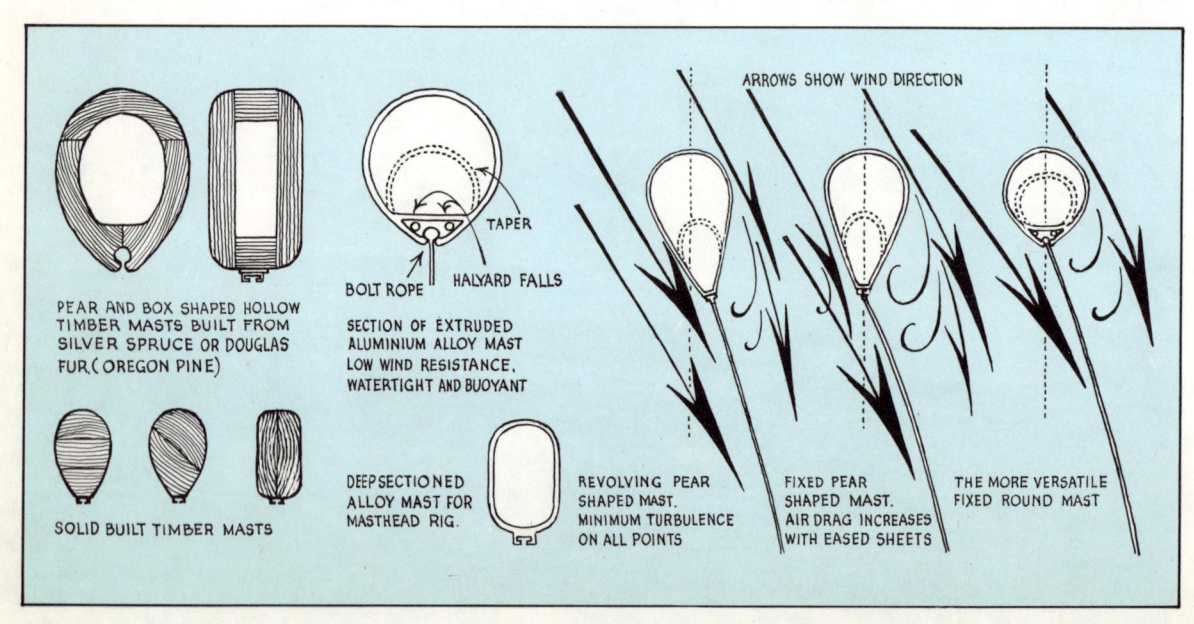

It has been consistently proved that round, alloy masts, slightly flattened on the after side, with sail tracks extruded as an integral part for small boats and pop-riveted on for small yachts, have much better air flow around them and are a lot better for bending. Most Australian champion boats of the small classes—Moths, Gwen 12s, Lightweight Sharpies, Flying Dutchmen and 505s—have masts of the former type. This latest trend in almost round, flexible masts has spread overseas from Australia; in fact, outstanding craft in many countries have masts first designed in Australia. And perhaps underlining it all is the fact that the 5.5-metre gold medal winner *Barranjoey*, of Australia, carried an almost round mast in the Tokyo Olympic Games. She was tried with a pear-shaped mast after winning the Australian selection trials but Bill Northam and his crew discarded it in favour of her old, round mast.

We have been considering, of course, masts suitable for bending. For boats with masts that are rigged to remain straight, round sections, slightly flattened on the after side, are desirable to induce better wind flow. But from a practical point of view, especially for masthead-rigged yachts, it is most desirable to have rigid masts slightly oval in section since this gives them much greater strength fore-and-aft where they are supported only by a forestay and backstay. They do not need to have so much strength laterally because they are well supported by the side shrouds.

Thus, as a corollary, the overall perimeter of an oval-shaped, rigid mast, particularly in the upper sections, does not need to be as great as that of a round mast to attain the same strength. So we must learn to compromise, balancing the disadvantages of disturbed air flow around the mast against advantages of having a spar that is of smaller volume and, because it can be lighter towards the top, one that exerts less leverage and makes the boat more stable.

When you have mastered or at least become thoroughly familiar with all the theory and practice that Jack Earl and I have tried to provide in the preceding pages, you should be a reasonably competent hand in a boat.

Certainly you should have learnt that this noble pastime of sailing is a constant challenge to your ingenuity, skill and attention to detail and that beyond all other physical endeavours it returns bountiful dividends in pleasure and good health for every ounce of effort you put into it. Good sailing!

# Major knots

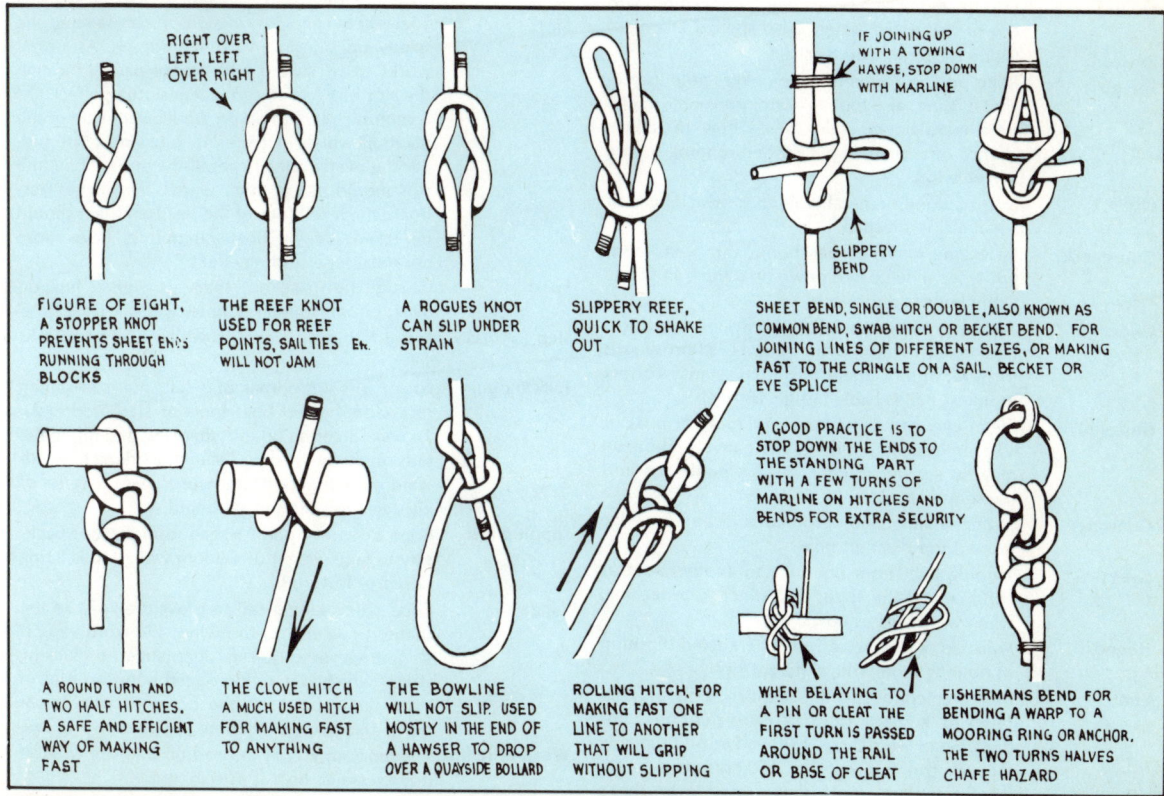

FIGURE OF EIGHT, A STOPPER KNOT PREVENTS SHEET ENDS RUNNING THROUGH BLOCKS

THE REEF KNOT USED FOR REEF POINTS, SAIL TIES Etc. WILL NOT JAM — RIGHT OVER LEFT, LEFT OVER RIGHT

A ROGUES KNOT CAN SLIP UNDER STRAIN

SLIPPERY REEF, QUICK TO SHAKE OUT

SHEET BEND, SINGLE OR DOUBLE, ALSO KNOWN AS COMMON BEND, SWAB HITCH OR BECKET BEND. FOR JOINING LINES OF DIFFERENT SIZES, OR MAKING FAST TO THE CRINGLE ON A SAIL, BECKET OR EYE SPLICE. IF JOINING UP WITH A TOWING HAWSE, STOP DOWN WITH MARLINE. SLIPPERY BEND

A ROUND TURN AND TWO HALF HITCHES. A SAFE AND EFFICIENT WAY OF MAKING FAST

THE CLOVE HITCH A MUCH USED HITCH FOR MAKING FAST TO ANYTHING

THE BOWLINE WILL NOT SLIP. USED MOSTLY IN THE END OF A HAWSER TO DROP OVER A QUAYSIDE BOLLARD

ROLLING HITCH, FOR MAKING FAST ONE LINE TO ANOTHER THAT WILL GRIP WITHOUT SLIPPING

WHEN BELAYING TO A PIN OR CLEAT THE FIRST TURN IS PASSED AROUND THE RAIL OR BASE OF CLEAT

A GOOD PRACTICE IS TO STOP DOWN THE ENDS TO THE STANDING PART WITH A FEW TURNS OF MARLINE ON HITCHES AND BENDS FOR EXTRA SECURITY

FISHERMANS BEND FOR BENDING A WARP TO A MOORING RING OR ANCHOR. THE TWO TURNS HALVES CHAFE HAZARD

**Conversion Table**
1 inch = 2.54 centimetres
1 foot = 30.48 centimetres
3.281 feet = 1 metre
1 square foot = 0.0929 square metres
x square feet ÷ 10.764 = y square metres
1 nautical mile = 1.853 kilometres
1 knot (nautical miles p/h) = 1.853 kph

# Glossary  Sailing Terms

**Back:** To haul a sail to windward to stop the boat or to help turn her away from the wind.

**Block:** Case or shell of wood, metal or plastic with a sheave (grooved wheel) through which a rope runs. Double blocks have two sheaves.

**Bolt rope:** Rope reinforcement around edge of sail; usually sewn on to port side as guide to handling in dark; headsails now are commonly wired to prevent distortion and mainsails reinforced with synthetic fibre tape.

**Boom:** Spar of wood or tubular metal holding foot of sail, usually mainsail. Spinnaker boom (or spinnaker pole) projects the for'ard corner of spinnaker.

**Brace:** Rope or wire (on large yachts) rigged to spinnaker pole to control its fore and aft position. Should be same as spinnaker sheet to facilitate gybing.

**Camber (or Draught):** Fullness of a sail created by sailmaker. This can be altered by bending middle of mast forward and bending boom downwards.

**Cap shroud:** Wire led from either side of mast over spreader down to side deck to support upper section of spar.

**Cat rig:** Single sail rigged on mast that is stepped well forward in a boat.

**Clew:** Aftermost corner of a sail.

**Cringle:** Eye made of rope worked into edge or clew of sail with a ring or oval of metal inside it.

**Draft:** Extreme depth of a boat's hull (with centreboard down) below the water. (Also spelled Draught.)

**Fairlead:** Guide for rope, wire or chain.

**Foreguy:** Rope or wire rigged from spinnaker pole to prevent it rising; also rope (or wire) preventer rigged from main boom end towards bow to reduce chance of accidental gybe when running square before wind.

**Gaff:** Spar of wood or metal tube on to which head of a gaff sail is attached.

**Gooseneck:** Swivelling joint between boom and mast. Modern types slide up and down on a track and have a number of adjustments.

**Gripe:** Tendency of boat to head up into the wind; less rake in mast, thus moving centre of effort of sails forward, or movement of weight aft may correct it, unless hull is badly designed.

**Gudgeon:** Metal eye set into transom (or tuck) of boat to take pintle set into rudder; alternatively, gudgeon may be set into rudder to take pintle set into transom (or tuck).

**Gunwale:** Strengthening and protective wooden edge around top plank of boat.

**Gybe:** Turning boat from one tack to another so that wind crosses the stern; as distinct from tacking, when wind crosses bow.

**Hounds:** Point on mast where shrouds are fixed. Position of hounds varies with different rigs.

**Knot:** Measurement of speed. Sea miles per hour. One refers to 'X knots' *not* to 'X knots per hour'. Application of word 'knot' to speed arose originally through counting number of knots (tied at set lengths in long rope) that passed over ship's stern during a set time.

**Leech:** Aftermost edge of a sail.

**Leeward:** (Pronounced Looward.) Anything that is in a downwind direction. For instance, the leeward side of the boat, leeward rigging, a ship to leeward.

**Leeway:** Sideways slide of a boat. Every sailing boat makes some.

**Luff:** To come head to wind, or (as noun), the leading edge of a sail.

**Mainsheet horse:** Arched bar with ends bolted through deck; or a length of strong wire with the ends shackled to deck; or a metal or strong plastic track bolted or screwed to deck. In each case it runs across (athwart) the deck from port to starboard and carries lower mainsheet block, allowing this to slide to leeward side. A modern mainsheet horse has a roller-bearing traveller to which lower mainsheet block is shackled. There are also 'stops' on the horse to enable sheet block to be fixed at a number of positions.

**Masthead rig:** When headsail is hoisted to the masthead.

**Rake:** Angle at which a mast is set from vertical. Most masts are raked slightly aft to give boats a tendency to weather helm, but if this is excessive it may often be reduced by lessening the rake until mast is upright, if necessary. Very few masts are raked forward.

**Roach:** Precisely, the hollow or concave curve in the foot of a squaresail but, through common usage, a convex curve in the edge of a sail (which should, to be precise, be called 'round').

**Seaway:** Broken or rough water outside a harbour.

**Sheet:** Rope that controls the set or trim of a sail.

**Shrouds:** Wire side supports of a mast; fore and aft supports are called stays.

**Shy:** Term usually refers to spinnaker set with pole rigged forward for a reaching breeze.

**Slot:** Space between leeward side of mainsail and the windward side of an overlapping jib. As a boat works to windward and breeze passes through the slot it is said to produce a slotting effect, i.e. a venturi stream of air on the leeward side of the mainsail which increases its efficiency. The bigger the overlap of a headsail the more 'open' the slot should be; in other words, the further outboard the lead block of the headsail sheet should be taken. Beamy boats, therefore, have more potential for a slotting effect.

**Spar:** Usually the mast, but spars in general include mast, boom, spinnaker pole, whisker pole.

**Step (of mast):** Metal frame or socket in which heel of mast is set.

**Tack (noun):** Lower forward corner of a sail; point of sailing of a close-hauled boat (port or starboard tack). *To tack:* Steering up into the wind and filling the sails on the other side. *Tacking:* working to windward by steering on alternate courses (a series of zig-zags) to port and starboard.

**Topping lift:** Rope or wire support rigged from mast or backstay to take weight of a boom while sail is being raised or lowered.

**Vang:** Rope controlling a sail to prevent a twist in the shape it presents to the wind; the word vang is sometimes used as an alternative to 'kicking strap', which is a tackle rigged between foot of mast and a point on the boom to stop boom rising and twist developing in upper part of sail.

**Weather helm:** Tendency of a boat to head up into the wind. If it is excessive boat is said to 'gripe'.

**Whisker pole:** Short spar of wood or metal tube for booming out jib when running downwind.

**Windward:** Anything that is in an upwind direction. For instance, the windward side of the boat, windward rigging, a ship to windward.

**Yaw or Yawing:** To sail an unsteady course.

Setting a spinnaker

Spinnaker trimming

Gybing and lowering a spinnaker

Sails and sail handling

Setting up the mainsail

Leech adjustments

Camber of mainsails

Adjusting mainsheet — light conditions

Adjusting mainsheet — fresh conditions

Headsails and their uses

Overlapping headsails

Setting up headsails

Shape of headsails

Trimming headsails

Masts

Heavy winds

Backstay adjustments

Controlling mast bends

Side bends

Mast shapes